D0193934

Is This Your Idea of a Good Time, God?

Discovering Yourself in Biblical Stories

Other books & resources by Ralph Milton

God for Beginners
The Family Story Bible (formerly, *Living God's Way*)
Man to Man
Sermon Seasonings
Angels in Red Suspenders
Julian's Cell
The Essence of Julian
The Great Canadian Improv Bible Study

Ralph Milton

Illustrations by Richard Caemmerer Jr.

Is This Your Idea of a Good Time, God?

Discovering Yourself in Biblical Stories

WoodLake

Editing: Jim Taylor, Michael Schwartzentruber
Design: Lois Huey Heck
Cover Design: Lois Huey Heck
Consulting art director: Robert MacDonald
Illustrations: Richard Caemmerer

WoodLake is an imprint of Wood Lake Publishing, Inc. Wood Lake Publishing acknowledges the financial support of the Government of Canada, through the Book Publishing Industry Development Program (BPIDP) for its publishing activities. Wood Lake Publishing also acknowledges the financial support of the Province of British Columbia through the Book Publishing Tax Credit.

At Wood Lake Publishing, we practice what we publish, being guided by a concern for fairness, justice, and equal opportunity in all of our relationships with employees and customers. Wood Lake Publishing is an employee-owned company, committed to caring for the environment and all creation. Wood Lake Books recycles, reuses, and encourages readers to do the same. Resources are printed on 100% post-consumer recycled paper and more environmentally friendly groundwood papers (newsprint), whenever possible. A percentage of all profit is donated to charitable organizations.

Canadian Cataloguing in Publication Data
Milton, Ralph
Is This Your Idea of a Good Time, God?

ISBN 1–55145–068–2
1. Bible stories, English. I. Title.
BS550.2.M54 1995   220.9'505   C95–910708–8

Copyright © 1995, 2005, 2006 Ralph Milton
All rights reserved. No part of this publication may be reproduced –
except in the case of brief quotations embodied in critical articles and reviews –
stored in an electronic retrieval system, or transmitted in any form or by any means,
electronic, mechanical, photocopying, recording, or otherwise, without
prior written permission of the publisher or copyright holder.

Published by
Wood Lake Books, Inc.
9025 Jim Bailey Road
Kelowna, BC, V4V 1R2
www.woodlakebooks.com

10 9 8 7 6
Printed in Canada by
Blitzprint

To
Jacob Daniel

CONTENTS

The Prodigal son's mother

About this book

This is a very different approach to the Bible. To understand how it is different, please read *First, you fall in love*, on pages 9–36.

This book can generate some very unique Bible study experiences. To find out about that, please read the *Study Guide* titled *Finding new friends in the Bible*, on pages 185–192.

I tell 23 stories in this book, beginning on page 39. Each of them has four sections:

1. *a few words of introduction*, usually with a bit of historical or biblical background, just enough to give you the context;
2. *a paraphrase of the story in the Bible.* While this is a less formal presentation than you find in the Bible, I have tried to stick to the story as it is told there. In a few cases I've left out some unnecessary details;
3. *an explanation of why I wrote the story* and where I am coming from. Implied in each of these is, I hope, the idea that you would imagine another story that fits your experience;
4. *a story* that
    a) may be only very loosely connected to the biblical text,
    b) may simply retell the biblical story with a slightly different slant, or
    c) may leave you wondering, "Where did he come up with that?"

First, you fall in love
a new way to enjoy the Bible

Starving at the dinner table

"Life is a banquet," said Aunt Mame, "and most damn fools are starving to death."

I thought of that famous quotation during a talk show at a local radio station. Another sociological study somewhere had reported that the mainline churches were slip-sliding into oblivion. The local radio station – which normally gives religion about as much respect as a dog gives a fire hydrant – suddenly decided that the churches were news. They called me for an interview.

Nothing gets the media salivating as much as a good sex scandal in the church, but if you can't have that, then a survey showing that the church is in its death throes will do. And so those of us who are sometimes "spokes-folks" for the church get hauled in to respond to unanswerable questions such as, "Why aren't more people coming to church?"

Well, the fact is, lots of people *are* coming to church. More people go to church on a single Sunday than attend major sports events in a year. The problem is not whether people are attending church or not. The problem is, are they *hearing* anything that makes a real difference to their lives when they come?

Depending on which survey you quote, the vast majority of people in North America describe themselves as Christian, and an even larger group call themselves "spiritual." About 25% go to church with some degree of regularity. So why do the media folks seem so convinced that the church is dead – or at least so close to death that they can record its final death rattle on video tape?

Sam Keen points out that only 2% of us ever talk about matters of faith with our best friends or members of our family. Our faith, says Keen, "is as superficial as it is extensive." (Sam Keen, *Hymns to an Unknown God*, p.11, Bantam Books, 1994) Maybe the media folk are on to something after all. They never hear us talk about our faith over coffee at the office. They never hear us getting excited about spiritual realities. They smell a rat. They may be wiser than I give them credit for.

Taken for granted

Walter Brueggemann offers this perspective:

The preacher in U.S. culture deals with a claim that is commonly accepted as truth by the listeners. That is, we preach mostly to believers.

There is a casual, indifferent readiness, even in our increasingly secularized society, to grant the main claims of the gospel – not to grant them importance, but [simply] to accept them as premises of religious life. In fact, it is precisely the problem for the proclamation of the gospel that the great claims of the gospel do not seem to be problematic or in question.

The gospel is too readily heard and taken for granted, as though it contained no unsettling news and no great threat. What began as news in the gospel is easily assumed, slotted, and conveniently dismissed. We depart having heard, but without noticing the urge to transformation that is not readily compatible with our comfortable believing that asks little and receives less. (Walter Brueggemann, *Finally Comes The Poet, p.1, Fortress Press, 1989*)

I go to church pretty well every Sunday. Sometimes I read the scripture lesson. As a sometime TV performer, I've learned to look up from my script now and then, to meet the eyes of the listeners. So I look up and see the faces of the folks sitting there neatly in rows, and I know, beyond any shadow of doubt, that most of them are thinking about something else. If I ask them why (and I do), they say, "The Bible is something we leave to the preachers to fuss over. It's much too complicated for us anyway. Let them tell us what it's all about."

What happened?

Something has gone haywire.

The Protestant Reformation was all about getting the Bible into the hands of ordinary people. My Mennonite forebears *died* for the right to be able to read the Bible themselves; the same can be said for people in almost any faith tradition. Many of us trace our roots to ancestors who left everything in Europe in order to come to a country where they would have freedom of religion. And the symbol of that freedom was the right to read the Bible for themselves.

What happened? Why do we leave the Bible to the clergy to interpret for us? How did it happen that we gave away the thing our forebears fought and died for?

A mystery writer (P.D. James, perhaps, or Josephine Tey, who did a dandy novel about the mystery of King Richard III) could make a great thriller out of that process. I'm certainly not in their league, but even I can sketch out a hypothetical conspiracy. It would go something like this.

How Christians lost the Bible

The story begins during the Reformation, somewhere in Europe.

The Bible is owned by the Bishops. It is chained down in the cathedrals and only the privileged few are allowed access. Priests and monks, mostly. The Church reserves for itself the right to interpret Holy Scripture.

Then the unwashed masses, their passions inflamed by red-eyed reformers, storm the gothic fortresses and take the Bible for their own.

The beleaguered Bishops huddle in their palaces. "We must rescue the Bible from those madding throngs," quoth the head Bishop. "Those people will come to all kinds of wrong conclusions. We've got to get the Bible back under our control."

"But how?" quoth Bishop #2. "There are too many of them. They have the power of numbers. And they have among them scholars, intellectuals, who argue eloquently that the Bible rightly belongs to the people."

"Ha!" quoth the head Bishop. "Kung Fu!"

"Huh?" quoth Bishop #2.

"The ancient oriental art of self defense. You use the power of your enemy to defeat your enemy."

"Huh?" quoth Bishop #2.

"The scholars, you idiot," quoth the head Bishop. "We get those scholars to explain the scriptures to the masses. We'll sponsor the scholars – hell, we'll *pay* the scholars – so they do lots of learned commentaries, in-depth studies, complex exegesis and a whole pile of study guides that only they really understand. We'll encourage them to invent words like 'transubstantiation' and 'hermeneutics'..."

"Herman who?" quoth Bishop #2.

"...and we'll organize the clergy as a kind of junior scholars' league who will learn the big words and sprinkle their sermons with unintelligible quotations. That will have the net effect of convincing people that only scholars and clergy can understand the Bible."

"Huh?" quoth Bishop #2.

"People can *own* all the Bibles they want. They'll never read them. We'll get them so spooked they'll think you need three years of seminary to understand the Bible. Am I brilliant or am I brilliant?"

Bishop #2 sucked his episcopal ring for a minute. "But the clergy. Won't they try to get people interested in the Bible?"

"Oh sure. And we'll encourage that. But clergy are human, after all, and they'll want to use all that stuff they learned in seminaries. They'll use the same approach and the same concepts and categories their professors used on them. That'll either scare people off or bore them to tears."

"Brilliant," quoth Bishop #2.

Dismembered or pickled?

The conspiracy theory is just plain silly. Or, on the other hand, maybe it isn't.

Wood Lake Books did a bit of a survey a couple of years ago. The survey discovered what others who have done similar surveys already knew. Many, many churches have no Bible study going on at all. In fact, this is probably true of *most* of the mainline churches. Even in churches which *do* hold Bible studies, most lay people don't participate. The most common reason given is that they don't want to be embarrassed by having their lack of biblical knowledge exposed. They are convinced that the Bible is important, but only clergy really have the training to understand it. So it's safer to leave the Bible alone.

Harvey Cox makes some interesting observations in *Religion in the Secular City.* Protestants lost the Bible in two ways, says Cox.

First, the historical-critical method of biblical analysis effectively took the Bible out of the hands of lay people and put it into the hands of the scholars.

As a reaction to that loss, the fundamentalists grabbed it back from the scholars. They insisted that everything in the Bible had equal value. Every word was just as true as every other word. The begats and the Beatitudes were all on the same level. They allowed all sorts of eccentric interpretations, reducing the Bible to what Cox calls "a kind of *I-Ching*," a crystal ball that will reveal everything you want to know as long as you peer into it the right way. So instead of giving the liberating message of the Bible into the hands of ordinary folk, the fundamentalists removed it as much as the scholars had.

Reacting to the fundamentalists, the scholars dug in with their detailed explanations. Reacting to the scholars, the fundamentalists claimed more and more for the Bible. First infallibility. Then inerrancy. Then...

Ordinary folks simply felt more confused, more left out.

The result? Liberal scholars "dismembered" the Bible, says Cox, and the fundamentalists "embalmed it." He says, and I concur, "It must be given back to the ordinary people from whom all these well-meaning authorities have removed it."

Boring, boring!

There's another reason why ordinary people don't actually read the Bible themselves. Many folks are convinced the Bible is boring. With some justification. The Bible is often presented in the most mind-numbing manner possible.

Listen to a typical lay person, or, for that matter, most clergy, reading the Bible aloud in church. If they read bedtime stories to their children that badly, their kids would hate the book, regardless of what it was about.

We have a sorry history to overcome. I'm as guilty of contributing to that history as anyone. Many years ago, I taught a group of eight-year-old boys Sunday school in the furnace room at East Trail United Church. I'm sure I managed to persuade those boys to make a lifetime commitment never to look inside the Bible or appear inside a church again.

I wish I'd had something like *The Whole People of God* or *Seasons of the Spirit* curriculum at the time. The writers of those curriculum turn themselves inside out to make the Bible lively, interesting, and relevant. They work hard to get the kids involved in the stories. They have the kids act out the stories. They draw pictures. They make puppets. They sing lively songs. But what about us adults?

As a society, we have this wrong-headed conviction that people grow up. We don't. Our toys may get more expensive, but most of us are really still big kids – and the ones who aren't, aren't any fun to be with. And if we're just big kids, then the educational principles that apply to six-year-olds also apply to 60-year-olds like me.

Which is why the children's time in church, if it's well done, is usually the most interesting and beneficial part of the service for the adults.

A conspiracy of silence

Given that history, it's not too surprising that lay people park the old family Bible on the bookshelf and leave it there to gather dust.

I've led a number of Bible study groups in my home church. In the very first session, I tell folks that I don't believe everything in the Bible. I tell them there are parts of the Bible that have little if any significance for people living several thousand years later, and there are other parts that are plain wrong, and sometimes outright evil.

For instance, I don't believe that God commanded King Saul to attack the Amalekites and "kill both man and woman, child and infant, ox and sheep, camel and donkey" (1 Samuel 15:3). I have no doubt the biblical writers *thought* God said that, but I think they got it wrong. And I believe that the God I worship, the God who loves and cares for all humanity and all creation, wants me to use my head and my instincts and wants me to argue with the scripture at that point, and many others.

We do that already, I point out. Very few of us today believe that the stories of creation, as told in the Bible, are a historical account of the way things actually happened. Why, then, do we get nervous if somebody talks back to St. Paul?

When I explained my attitude, the folks in the Bible study groups heaved a palpable sigh of relief. Most of them were convinced their ministers believed every single word in the Bible. So, while they were in church, they pretended they believed every word too. But they were educated, intelligent folk. And so in fact they were quietly accepting what made sense to them, and setting the rest aside. They felt guilty about not being able to believe much of what was in the Bible so they just kept quiet. They never talked about it with each other or with their minister. The whole business was embarrassing!

In every case, I knew the minister of the church quite well. Their minister was Bev Milton, to whom I am married. I knew Bev did not read the Bible that way. I knew that most of the other clergy, friends and colleagues of Bev's, did not read the Bible that way either. When I told these clergy what the folks in the Bible study group had said, they threw their hands up in frustration. "I've never been a biblical literalist," they complained. "And I've said so over and over in the pulpit. When I reflect on a biblical text during a sermon, I never suggest that people should hear it as a historical or scientific document. Where did people get that?"

Beats me. But there it is.

It's one of those unintentional "conspiracies" that happen. Perhaps those folks in the Bible study groups heard the occasional TV evangelist approach the Bible as the literal "word of God." Perhaps that's how they were taught as children. Certainly, when the popular media touch the subject, they assume that all Christians think of the Bible as having been dictated by God into the ear of a scribe who simply wrote it down, word for word. They assume this even though you have to go pretty far to the right end of the religious spectrum before you find clergy who believe that. But that's a popular perception – and perceptions are reality.

Several of my church friends drove about 100 kilometers one evening to hear a lecture by Bishop John Shelby Spong, who wrote the book *Rescuing the Bible from Fundamentalism* (among others). Spong elaborated on the same points about the Bible that I've just made. These friends, all of whom had been going to fairly liberal churches for most of their adult lives, were intrigued. They hadn't heard this kind of thing before. One of them, a woman who has been elected to a number of highly responsible regional church positions, was quite angry. "Why have our clergy never *told* us this before?" she demanded.

Well, they had. But she hadn't heard. And neither had most of the folks who sat beside her in church. But the essential elements of what Spong was saying have been taught in our seminaries and theological schools since the beginning of the century. But somehow they haven't made it through to most of us laypeople.

Getting the Bible back

As lay people, we've lost the Bible. We've lost the confidence to read it for ourselves; we've lost the courage to argue with it. So it sits on the shelves in our homes gathering dust.

We need to take the Bible back. Most clergy are more than willing – in fact they'd be delighted – to give it back to us. Admittedly, not all clergy know *how* to do that. But as with most freedoms, nobody can *give* us the Bible. We have to take it.

That "taking back," according to Cox and others, has happened in a few places through a phenomenon called "liberation theology."

"Liberation theology" refers to a movement in the hearts and minds and lives of people. People sit down together, read the Bible together, hear the stories, and fall in love with the characters in those stories. They talk about those stories, wrestle with the implications, argue with the text sometimes, and let the Bible speak to them in their lives. Then, fired up and focused, they go out and live the convictions that have taken shape in their hearts and minds.

The epicenter of this movement was among the battered and suffering people of Central and South America. Not in the megachurches or seminaries, but in the village huts, among people who read the Bible laboriously, word by word – people who had no access to commentaries or study guides. They had no clergy, no scholars, to tell them what it all meant. They had to figure it out for themselves. And they did.

They heard the stories. They heard the songs. They retold the stories in their own words and used the images and metaphors of their own lives. They found *themselves* in the stories and the songs. They found a liberating insight and proceeded to live it out. That liberating insight was creative, innovative, relevant, and often politically radical.

When church leaders in North America heard of this movement, they said, "Hey, this stuff is good. Everyone should know about this. I wonder if we could get the folks in our suburban churches to approach the Bible this way?"

Their intentions were good. But they made the same old mistakes all over again. They gave the movement a name. Liberation Theology. That made it about as useful as pink celluloid fire tongs. The name alone took most of the life out of it. Who would want to be part of anything with a dry name like Liberation Theology?

Then they analyzed and categorized and systematized and wrote books with long words and many footnotes and said to the Christians of North America, "Here! This is great stuff."

But what they showed us resembled the living experience of the folk in Latin America about as much as a can of tuna resembles the magnificent fish that leaps out of the sea.

"Huh?" said the Christians of North America.

The sad thing is that the church leaders, the clergy, and the scholars genuinely *want* ordinary folk to read and understand the Bible. They agonize and grieve that so few people share the tradition, the story, the faith that moves them. They work hard and carefully. But their training is mostly academic. And they make the classic mistake of imposing their own categories and systems and styles on a tradition, a mythology, that is disorganized and messy and wonderfully, creatively naive.

For the Bible is not, and never has been, a careful, logical, rational, exposition of a theory. It's the real-life encounters of real live people with a real living God who refuses to be put in a pigeonhole. As a result, the Bible is, as I said, disorganized and messy and wonderfully, creatively, naive.

But the seminaries take all this messiness, this topsy-turvy jumble of inexplicable experiences, and dissect it the way my high school English teacher used to dissect poems and my biology teacher dissected frogs. By the time they were finished, both the poems and the frogs were cold and dead. From the seminaries, the preachers take their dissected message out to the folks in the churches, and the folks in the churches say, "Huh? Well, I guess so. You're the doctor!"

We're back at square one.

A tale of turkeys

The fact is, we need both the experts and the ordinary people. The Bible is the single most important book in the Christian world. We'd be crazy not to have scholars studying it. We'd be crazy not to have people taking it seriously – so seriously they're willing to let it govern their lives.

But we're also crazy if we leave the Bible to the scholars or the fanatics. If that "single most important book" is worth anything at all, it has to live in our own lives, too.

It's a "both/and" rather than an "either/or" matter.

Sometimes I'm asked to preach in church services. But it's more fun when I'm asked to take the children's time. One time, with the kids gathered around me on the chancel steps, I asked them, "What's the big difference between turkeys and people?"

My dad used to raise turkeys in southern Manitoba. We talk about that. Soon the children and I have agreed that turkeys have a well-deserved reputation for stupidity.

The responses to my question are varied and wonderful. Eventually I point out that turkeys have their eyes on the sides of their heads. They have *mon*ocular vision. We humans have our eyes on the front, side by side, so that we can look at the same object with two eyes at the same time. We have *bin*ocular vision. Because of that, humans have depth perception. Turkeys do not.

To demonstrate, the kids and I play a game. "Close one eye." I demonstrate, of course. "Stick one hand out as far in front of you as you can and point a finger up to the ceiling. Then with your other hand, come at your finger *from the side*, and see if you can touch one finger to the other."

They can't do it – not on the first try, at least. Working from only one eye, one viewpoint, they lose their depth perception.

Then I suggest to them that, just as two eyes work better than one, so do two viewpoints. I get some of the children to stand behind me, and tell the children in the front what they see. Invariably, to the great glee of the congregation, one of them mentions my bald spot. Someone looking at me from the front sees only a full head of hair. But two people, looking from different directions, get a more complete picture of my incomplete thatch.

Two people with two different viewpoints have another advantage that turkeys don't have. They can talk to each other. They can share their insights. Granted, this revelation is not likely to be written up in the *History of the World's Greatest Ideas* and children over the age of ten often are looking a bit bored.

"You know that already, don't you?"

"Yeah," they mumble.

So I turn the tables on them. I do a quick opinion poll. "How many of you think *Deep Space Nine* (or any other currently popular program) is cool?"

A few hands go up.

"And how many think it sucks?"

A few other hands go up.

It's time for the punch line. "You are both right. Because each of you sees it from a different perspective."

It's a hard sell to get kids – or adults, for that matter – to realize that two people can experience the same thing and come away with totally different impressions, and that both of them may be right. People tend to see the world through one turkey eye and say, "That's it. That's reality! This is the way I see it, and if you disagree with me, you must be wrong." In its religious form, that attitude is called fundamentalism.

Two eyes, two brains

We humans have a left brain and a right brain. Generally, the left brain takes care of logical, rational stuff, like figuring out your income tax and getting to work on time and driving your car by the rules of the road. The right brain has the creative, emotional things to look after, such things as singing songs, making love, laughing, admiring a rainbow, or enjoying a good meal with friends. It's an oversimplification, but the left brain takes things apart to understand them, and the right brain puts things together to experience them.

And we need *both* sides of our brains to function. Take a meal with friends as an example. When you're cooking it, you read the recipe and follow the directions with your left brain, but then you sit down and enjoy the meal with your right brain. If your right brain shut down, you'd be an emotionless robot. If your left brain shut down you'd be a smiling idiot. A whole, well-balanced human uses *both* sides of the brain.

It's surprising how often that concept escapes the most intelligent folks. If it's not logical and rational it's not real. If you can't count it, it's not worth having. Our society and our church tends to value left-brained thinking far more than right-brained.

Right-brained artistic types like me make a similar mistake, of course. I often look down my considerable nose at "technocrats," and argue that if it isn't a story or a poem or a painting or a song, it's got no value.

We need *both*. We need two eyes to see depth and perspective. We need each other to hear how things look through other eyes. And we need both sides of our brain to experience God's word. This essay, then, is not a plea for one or the other, but for balance.

Like those monocular turkeys, I find it much too easy to assume that my own individual perspective is the only one and that everything would be fine if the rest of the world would just see reality the way I do.

What has all that got to do with the Bible? Just this – any Bible study that is going to work has to use both sides of the brain.

Chained down to keep it safe

Don't get me wrong. I am not calling biblical scholars and clergy a bunch of turkeys. They are caring, conscientious, and intelligent women and men. The last thing they want is to keep the Bible away from people. No, that's the *second* last thing. The last thing they want is to have people get it *wrong*. Like the fictional Bishop in my little conspiracy farce, they don't want people coming to the wrong conclusions and hence the wrong theology.

Since the first scribes began writing down scriptures 3,000 years ago, there have been recurring attempts to control and interpret. Some of these were organized, planned, deliberate attempts to keep the Bible out of the hands of ordinary folk. The Bibles really were chained down in the churches prior to the Reformation, partly because they were so valuable (they were all hand-written) but also to keep them out of the hands of the unwashed masses.

That's not our problem anymore. We can buy a Bible in almost any bookstore, and often we can choose from a dozen or more translations. The problem infecting North American churches right now is more insidious. Everyone seems to agree, "We need to get folks reading the Bible for themselves." But what we do in our churches – and perhaps more significantly, what we *don't* do – has the net effect of making sure everyone owns a Bible but hardly anyone reads it.

Bubbling up

Yet Bible stories have a habit of popping up like grass through concrete. Church leaders keep trying to interest people in the Bible, and people keep coming back to try to figure out what this mysterious book is all about. Some study groups do an autopsy on the corpse given them by scholars, and some pore over the repair manual developed by the fundamentalists. They try really hard, but eventually get bored or frustrated and give up.

But those are not the only alternatives.

Here and there groups of people, most of them hurting people, get together and read the Bible, discover the stories, and see *themselves* in those stories. They fall in love with the people in those stories. As they connect their lives to those stories, they hear a liberating word and begin to live it. Some of those groups call themselves "blacks." Some call themselves "native." Some call themselves "feminist." Of course, they sometimes come to "wrong" conclusions. They're delightfully naive, sometimes. But they get excited by what they discover and it changes their lives. Sometimes it also puts enough fire into their bellies to go out and change those things they have found oppressive or dehumanizing.

You don't have to go to Latin America for examples. There's Iris.

I met Iris during one of many meetings I conduct with groups of clergy as I gather materials for a preaching periodical called *Aha!!!*. Some time ago, Iris began to imagine herself into the story of Mary Magdalene. Iris had a very unhappy childhood. She suffered from a number of illnesses complicated by family dysfunction. As a teenager, she often felt her life would count for very little, and she sometimes thought of suicide. Then she began to read herself into the painful life of Mary, who was cured of seven demons, who left her home and followed Jesus, and who became one of the great leaders of the early church. Iris found herself naming her own seven demons, seeking and finding a response to each one. Then she began to hear her own call as she imagined the way Jesus might have called Mary. Today, as a result of connecting her life to Mary Magdalene's, Iris is a happy and enthusiastic minister in the United Methodist Church.

Iris is one of thousands of women who have looked to the strong and the weak women in the Bible, imagined themselves into their lives, and gained insight and strength from doing so. Stories of the endurance and wit of Sarah, the resilience of Rebecca and Abigail, the leadership of Deborah, the pain of Tamar and Bathsheba, the courage of Esther, the suffering of Hagar, have changed lives.

Like many men, I have lived myself into the lives of Abraham the wanderer, Isaac whose name means "laughter," flat-footed Peter, and of course, Jesus of Nazareth. For me, the most helpful was the story of King David. In fact, I spent a couple of years imagining myself into the David story – exploring David as a cocky teenager, a successful young warrior, a troubled chief executive. David got into terrible hot water during a typical mid-life crisis. As a father, he was a failure until he lay on his deathbed. I put it all into a book about men's issues called *Man to Man* (Wood Lake Books, 1994). Of course I hope the book has helped other guys, but the guy who got the most out of the process was me.

The Bible made a difference to Iris and me and thousands of others because we allowed it to connect with our right brains. We fell in love with the people of the Bible. And as always happens when you fall in love, the one you love will change your life.

The "why" of it all

Please don't read this essay as a put-down of the careful, reasoned, and scholarly left-brain approach to the Bible. It is essential. If we don't have the left-brained approach to our life and to our Bible study, we're going to find ourselves in a dangerous mess. Without the left brain keeping track of things and asking annoying questions, religious faith flies off in the direction of the worst cults and sects.

Philosopher Sam Keen calls this left-brain ability his "bullshit detector." It gives us the capability to ask the hard and embarrassing questions. You don't have to look very far to see the kind of religious aberrations that happen when that left-brained capability is missing.

Nevertheless, there are things that cannot be understood rationally or logically. Isaac Asimov told the story of the eight-year-old boy who came home from school and told his mom about the sex education classes.

"So far," he said to his mother, "I've figured out what they do and how they do it. But I can't figure out why!"

The boy had the left-brain information. But he was missing the right-brain experiential stuff. He was not likely to understand the "why" of sex until the right combination of gonads and girlfriend brought him an insight that he'd never reach through study or analysis.

In storytelling workshops, I distinguish between three words: rational, irrational, and nonrational.

Rational thinking is careful and logical and systematic. *Irrational* is the direct opposite of that. *Nonrational* is neither.

Nonrational thinking makes perfect sense to those who have lived through an experience, but it is not necessarily logical or systematic. It may not even be consistent. It is thinking in another mode altogether.

You and I can stand on a hillside here in the Okanagan Valley where I live and see one of the rainbows, sometimes double and even triple rainbows, that happen after a summer afternoon rain. We will probably both agree that the rainbow is beautiful. Magnificent. Inspiring.

That is a nonrational judgment.

If either of us had a scientific background, we might describe the rainbow in terms of the refraction of light on water particles in the air. That would be a rational description, which doesn't in any way conflict with our nonrational agreement that the rainbow is beautiful.

On the other hand, if I go chasing across the valley in a frenzied attempt to find a pot of gold at the end of that rainbow, you might quite rightly say I was being irrational. I wasn't using either side of my brain.

Nonrational power

Dr. Martin Luther King was a fine scholar, a respected theologian, and an excellent social strategist. He could have offered learned lectures on the book of Exodus. He could also have offered analysis and statistics and case studies that would demonstrate beyond any rational doubt that black people were being oppressed in what was supposed to be the "land of the free."

That isn't what was needed in the 1960s, and it isn't what Dr. King offered. King knew that all over the U.S., black people had been raised on Bible stories told dramatically and powerfully by some of the best preachers and teachers in the world. King and many others sang the song: "Go down, Moses. Tell old Pharaoh—let my people go!" When King told that story of Moses, when he said, "I have been to the mountain top," he did not need to specify which mountain or explain "the promised land." The story of the Hebrews' escape from slavery put *nonrational power* into the civil rights movement.

Iris, who found her own life in the life of Mary Magdalene, didn't find it by doing a historical analysis of the role of the

Magdalene. She read the story just as it stands, then dreamed and imagined the details—including how Mary might have felt, and some of the conversations she might have had with Jesus. That gave her the power to change her life. After she entered seminary, she learned a lot more about Mary Magdalene and wrote a major paper on the subject. But *first* she allowed her nonrational self to love and to identify.

The story of King David, which has been so helpful to me personally, came to life for me as I retold the story in my own words, sometimes recasting the story in modern situations. Trying to imagine the details, the feelings, the nuances of the story, I found myself a part of it. Seeing how David destroyed so much of what had been important to him, when he had his mid-life crisis and raped Bathsheba, I was able to avoid that in my own mid-life crisis. But I stood on that rooftop with David, feeling my own impotence, feeling the temptation to compensate by overpowering another. That experience led eventually to some serious study of the history of King David, including a six-month sabbatical in Israel—but first I learned to love this complex man.

Falling in love

When Bev and I first met some 30-plus years ago, we took a decided dislike to each other. We were part of the same social group, so we saw each other from time to time, but basically ignored each other.

I had a car. Bev didn't. A mutual friend asked me to drive Bev to the hospital for some physio on her back. Whether it was chemistry or charisma, I'll never know, but suddenly I developed a very strong interest in this woman I had ignored. And she seemed to have an unusual interest in me. Over the years, we have read books, attended seminars, taken courses and counseling, and had a zillion conversations because we felt the need to know each other and ourselves better and to work on our relationship.

But *first, we fell in love.* Had it not been for the chemistry, or the charisma, or whatever it is that generates this kind of passion between two people, we certainly would not have bothered.

In the same way, we need to fall in love with some of the people of the Bible before we can even begin to study it meaningfully.

A love song

Anne Morrow Lindbergh began the modern ecological movement by writing *A Gift from the Sea*. Her book was a love song.

As a church we can best support the ecological movement by singing our half-forgotten love song to God's creation. If we could remember and sing our song we might woo others into a love affair with this planet. The necessary analysis and action will follow.

We Christians have been gifted with the legacy of a very old and exquisitely beautiful love song. The opening refrain is there in our scripture. "Behold, it was good!"

It is in loving creation that the church must show the way. It is in telling the old stories and the new stories, in singing the songs and doing the dance. It is in empowering, in making passionate the lovers – the church as a kind of holy aphrodisiac!

Like good yeast through bread dough

Fundamentally, I am optimistic. The spirit of those folks who read themselves into the Bible stories in Latin America, in black churches across the US, in feminist groups around the world – that spirit keeps bubbling like good yeast through bread dough. It isn't always encouraged or appreciated because folks who enjoy the Bible this way develop a very imaginative approach and can come up with some weird and wonderful ideas that normal Sunday-go-to-meetin' Christians don't always appreciate.

Did Mary of Magdala really dance on Pentecost day, the way I imagine in my story on page 177? No, of course the Bible doesn't say that. But then again, maybe she did.

Did the animals talk to God in the garden the way I describe it in my fantasy on page 42? No, that's not in the Bible either, but it's fun thinking about it.

Whether these stories are fact or fantasy is irrelevant. That's applying the rational approach again. The whole point of these stories is, first of all, to *enjoy* the Bible, to experience the Bible nonrationally.

There are significant numbers of places where Bible study groups get together to do just that. They enjoy the stories. They allow their imaginations to dance with the characters. They imagine what the individuals were like and how they felt. They wonder how they themselves might feel in that situation. They fall in love with the story, and discover insights and gain strength for their own lives. It's nonrational – and that's just fine as long as the rational is there to blow the whistle when somebody forgets this is a game of "let's pretend." It only becomes irrational when "let's imagine" gets treated as reality.

Often the clergy are part of those groups – in fact, they start many of them. I have an impression (which I can't prove) that it's mainly young female clergy who start such groups, though I also know of several situations where grey-bearded old fogies like me have stopped taking themselves quite so seriously and started dancing with the Bible.

A wonderful thing happens in those congregations. When a group gathers at the beginning of the week to play with the text the minister plans to preach on the next Sunday – to fall in love with it, and then to allow God's spirit, through their imaginations, to have its way with them, the sermon gets to be fun. It's more fun for the clergy who prepare it, and more meaningful for the folks who were part of the group. Sermons change from profound lectures into a sharing of life. The sermon stops being "Thus saith the Lord," or more accurately "Thus say the authorities," and becomes a loving, intimate conversation among people who are on a journey together.

In that kind of intimate conversation, hard things can be said. And heard. At least, those who wrestle and dance with the text are more able to hear the hard things. And when they talk to others in the congregation who didn't like what was said, they feel a connection with the preacher's message and so can help with the understanding.

"I'm finally putting into practice a theory they taught us in the homiletical courses," said one minister. "They always told us that preaching should arise out of the pastoral relationship, but they didn't give us any tools for making that happen. Well, this imaginative approach to Bible study really works."

The aggadah

Approaching the Bible with your creative and imaginative juices pumping (in other words, working from the right side of the brain) is not a new thing. It goes back well before the time of Jesus to a huge body of Jewish literature called the *Midrash*. Most of the *Midrash* is devoted to discussions, arguments, and interpretations of the *Torah* (the five books of the Law), but it's sprinkled with creative dreams and myths and speculations that are known collectively as *aggadah*.

Here's how the *Encyclopedia Judaica* describes *aggadah*.

Some of the exaggerations of the aggadah can be classed as fairy-tales, others are mainly witticisms, jokes, and pleasantries, or have merely served the rhetorical purpose of stimulating the interest of the people who came to listen to a sermon. To understand the *aggadot* [the plural of aggadah] the element of play and the poetic license of every creative storyteller and artist must be borne in mind.

[Historical aggadah] consists of additions and supplements to the Bible narrative and ancient *aggadot* preserved among the people, some dating back to Bible times themselves. Incidents and deeds only hinted at in Scripture serve as the kernels of dramatic accounts. Minor biblical figures become leading heroes. Biblical heroes become prototypes. For instance, Abraham is the archetype of all proselytizers, Esau the fashioner of violence and deceit. In aggadic history, the limitations of space and time are transcended and anachronisms abound. Shem [Noah's son] quotes Ecclesiastes and Isaiah, while Isaac obeys the Ten Commandments [written centuries after he lived]. Biblical heroes and their deeds are freed from the restraining bonds of time, the aggadic authors striving to discover in them meaning for their own and for the subsequent generations. (*Encyclopedia Judaica*, vol. 2, Keter Publishing House Jerusalem Ltd., POB 7145 Jerusalem, Israel, c. 1972.)

Jesus himself was, I think, a master of the *aggadah*. I see his liberal use of parables as evidence of that. In fact, if it hadn't been for the tradition of the *aggadah*, of adding to and embellishing the stories, I wonder how much of the Bible, including the New Testament, we'd have today.

And at that point, I find myself wondering how wisely we use the findings of biblical research, and to what extent scholars miss the point.

Is older always better?

There is an assumption behind virtually all biblical scholarship that the closer you get to the *original* text, the more *authentic* it is. It is probably true that, if you are looking for the historical underpinnings of the Bible, the older and more original material is the most accurate.

But I don't read the Bible primarily to learn history. I read it primarily because in doing so, I sometimes hear God whispering to me. In other words, my reasons for looking to the Bible are theological, not historical.

What troubles me is the unstated assumption in most biblical scholarship that if the text is older and more historically accurate, it must be more *faithful* to the will of God. That doesn't necessarily follow – not unless you're prepared to assume that God's spirit stopped speaking to us humans in 100 CE. Or 800 BCE. Or whenever the original stories began being told.

The original writer or storyteller may have missed the point of what God was trying to communicate. The Hebrew people did learn and grow through their various encounters with God, so later commentators and editors may well have heard God more clearly. Or less clearly.

This book you are holding has gone through a number of revisions, at my hands and others'. The final form is far more faithful to what I want to say than my original draft. Some books I have written have had the benefit of literally dozens of editors. The result was, I am convinced, much more faithful to the spirit of God than anything I could have done on my own. I think particularly of a collection of Bible stories retold for children, *The Family Story Bible,* which went through any number of drafts, and along the way was read by biblical scholars, educators, parents, and lots of children. Some suggested changing only a single word, but that word sometimes made a huge difference to the tone of the story.

The first texts of the Bible were oral folk literature, passed on from one generation to another. As they were passed on, details were changed. Some parts of the story were forgotten and other delightful stories were added. Some of them were borrowed from neighboring cultures. Some may have been imagined.

Presto! *Aggadah*!

A gold mine of insight

Some, such as the creation stories in Genesis, have their origins so far back in history that we can only guess at the source. We have no idea how often the original text was tinkered with or altered radically. Some alterations may have been deliberate; other times the storyteller may have forgotten the exact wording and simply fudged a bit.

But here's the miracle! The text as we have it now is a gold mine of spiritual insight!

I can imagine God hunkered down beside those desert campfires, whispering insight into the hearts of the storytellers so that gradually, over the years, the stories became more and more holy and less and less history. I believe our creating God was active in the hearts of the hard-working scribes who copied the text laboriously by hand – suggesting a more precise word here or a convenient omission there.

Does it offend you to think that God's spirit might have initiated a few rewrites of history because the meaning of the original event got bent in the telling? That's what I've done in the stories that follow – I've done some rewrites, based on what I think I hear God whispering into my heart. But would God do that? If the very idea offends you, reject it. If not, consider what that tells us about biblical history.

No, I'm not suggesting that God initiated every change anyone has ever made in the Bible. If we humans are given the freedom to make mistakes, we will make them. And we will make some of those mistakes while copying or translating the Bible. Some changes in the handed-down text were made for political reasons; some were just plain sloppiness. But if a creating God was involved in the original text, that holy creativity might well have entered into the revisions as well.

Inventing the Gospels

You might be willing to accept those concepts applied to the older Hebrew scriptures. Do you get nervous if I apply the same idea to the Christian scriptures? Well, I get nervous.

Scholars have been digging through the historical evidence and finding that less and less of the New Testament stands up to left-brain historical scrutiny. One of the most radical of these scholars is Burton Mack, who (among others) claims the historical roots of the gospels can be paired down to a collection of "Sayings of Jesus." Most of the historical material, he says, was invented by the early church. The first followers of Jesus didn't think of him as the Messiah – more like a Jewish Socrates.

"[The] challenge [of this research] is absolute and critical," says Mack. "It drives a wedge between the story as told in the narrative gospels and the history they are thought to record. The narrative gospels can no longer be read as the records of historical events that generated Christianity." (Burton L. Mack, *Lost Gospel, The Book of Q and Christian Origins*, HarperSanFrancisco)

Between people like Mack, the members of the "Jesus Seminar," and Bishop Spong, and others, there's lots of scholarly fuel scorching the historical roots of Christianity, to say nothing of the whole Judaic tradition. We may find that disturbing, but they are doing valuable work and we shouldn't be afraid of it. Their findings can add valuable insight and detail and meaning. They can force us to rediscover Jesus "again for the first time," as scholar Marcus Borg has suggested. If we stop fussing over the history, we hear God speak to us through the stories.

The Pentecost Spirit

I happen to believe there's more history to the Bible than Mack and Spong and others tell me there is but, as I said, I don't read the Bible primarily for the history. Even if there is very little history – even if all that wandering teacher named Jesus-bar-Joseph did was speak a few wise words and inspire enough people with enough enthusiasm so that the story of who he was and what he did began to grow – the New Testament would still be gospel, God's good news, to me.

And to some extent at least, some of it *was* invented. Or dreamed. Or imagined. Or hoped.

The story of Pentecost, as told in the second chapter of Acts, has something they called the "Holy Spirit" coming to the struggling little church 50 days after Jesus' crucifixion. They didn't know how to describe what happened to them in that upper room. They had to talk somehow about a sound in their minds *like* a mighty rushing wind, about auras *like* tongues of fire dancing among them. Perhaps it was in that Pentecost experience that God's spirit infected their imaginations to fill in the rest of the story, to imagine the details, to invent new incidents, to say over and over again, "Yes, this must have been so."

A good example is the story (in John 8:3–11) of the woman caught in adultery. Almost all scholars agree that this story was a later addition to the original Gospel of John. But isn't it a wonderful story? It is a *true* story, whether or not it ever happened. It is true because it speaks of a holy and enduring reality. I can well imagine some early scribe hearing that story and feeling, "Yes, Jesus would have done that. Jesus would have said that." And then he added the story to the manuscript being copied. And to that, the spirit of God would say, "Yes!"

God can speak to us through history, through fiction, through myth, and through a combination of all of them.

I believe our God is a creator whose spirit was part of the whole biblical process, prodding there, offering an insight here, applauding truth and discouraging falsehood. That creative process didn't stop when the last word of the Bible was written down. That same spirit calls us to bring our imagination to the text – our imagination and our lives. The "word" of God, ultimately, is not black marks on white paper or sounds we make with our mouths, but the faith we live.

Marcus Borg, in his book *Meeting Jesus Again for the First Time*, talks of hearing the Bible "in a state of postcritical naiveté – a state in which one can hear these stories as 'true stories' even while knowing that they are not literally true." He then goes on to cite an aboriginal American storyteller who always began telling his tribe's story of creation by saying, "Now I don't know if it happened this way or not, but I know this story is true."

How do I know there is genuine truth in those stories and legends? I don't. It is a nonrational approach to scripture. My ideas really say nothing, one way or another, about the historical-critical method used by most biblical scholars. They are two different ways of looking at the scripture. Like Marcus Borg, we need both scientific analysis and "postcritical naiveté." We aren't turkeys. We need *two* eyes to see the depth of truth that is there for us.

Like other artists, I have experienced the spirit of God unexpectedly bubbling up through my imaginings, coloring my inspirations, warming my words. I have spoken to artists in other media who share that experience. And I have seen it happening in storytelling groups where people opened themselves to that possibility.

If God's spirit can act through us, why not through the many good and not-so-good folk who handed the Bible down to us?

A church in trouble

You've probably heard the Sufi story of a *mullah* [a holy person] busily searching the ground outside the front of his house. Asked what he was looking for, he replied, "My button."

"Where did you lose it?" came the question.

"There, inside the house," he pointed.

"Then why are you looking here?"

"Because the light is so much better out here."

The ecumenical church seems haunted by a strange pointlessness. In presbyteries and dioceses and in national offices we struggle through issues and develop our positions. But we have a queasy feeling that the people in the pews and the rest of society don't give a damn. In our task forces and coalitions, we protest injustice and hear the hollow echo of our own voices. Pew sitters, and the folk outside the church, regard the larger church in the same way a jogger regards a yapping Pekingese behind a picket fence.

So we go back to our analysis of theological, ecclesiastical, and justice issues, hone them more sharply, articulate them more precisely, and hope somehow to lead and inspire.

We come up empty. Dry. We've left out the key ingredient. We're looking for our buttons in the wrong place.

Does God speak English?

In an address to the convocation of United Theological College in Montreal, Jim Taylor suggested that God does not speak English. Or any other language for that matter.

God speaks through our *experience*. Our personal experience, and our collective experience – which includes our perception of other people's experiences. For Christians, God speaks most powerfully through the experiences recounted in scripture. The Hebrew scriptures are a clear example of this almost self-evident truth.

We go to church feeling dried out spiritually, and often go home feeling even more desiccated. Little happens in church that gets us excited, worked up, enthusiastic, angry, or upset. There's not much to touch our emotions. We seldom connect with our everyday experiences. We hear words about God – but as Walter Brueggemann says, they sound more like a memo than a love song. They're a far cry from the "word" communicated through the passionate arts – myth, story, song, dance – or through Richard Caemmerer's powerful portraits that focus the stories in this book.

We are struggling desperately to find a spirituality of both power and wisdom. In the mainline churches we've relied mostly on the clear light of rational, analytical thinking. Let's not lose that, but let's add the warm, diffused light of nonrational intuition.

We have many things to learn from our native sisters and brothers. One of those lessons is that before anything significant can happen, we must take time to tell and to hear the stories – to love and respect the myths that help us know who we are and what we believe beyond the words we say. I use the word "know" as it is often used in the Hebrew scriptures: to "know" as a man and woman may know each other in love.

The lesson of our native people is the lesson of the Hebrew scriptures. It's there in Jesus' methods which are as instructive as his words. The Hebrews told stories and sang songs and lived lives. Jesus and his disciples were part of that tradition. They knew and loved their own songs and myths. Those myths were the "leaven" in their lives. Jesus built on those myths as he acted out the parable of his life.

A dangerous word

That word *myth* is dangerous, but I don't have a better one. In our everyday language, we usually use it to mean something that is untrue. I'm trying to use it the way anthropologists and sociologists use it – to mean a story or a ritual that helps us sense our own meaning intuitively. Some myths are legends, some are historically accurate. Historical myths tell of things that actually happened, but they are myths because there is meaning and significance in those stories that is greater than the historical facts.

A myth, as a little girl said, "is a story that is true on the inside."

Anne Squire, a prominent leader in The United Church of Canada, remembers an ordeal in the hospital. "I was having a very restless night with lots of pain. Suddenly I was absolutely sure that Christ was in the room with me holding my hand – there was no doubt in my mind whatsoever."

Anne learned the next night that the nurse had been there with her. The *outside,* objective truth of that story is that the duty nurse came in and held Anne's hand. But the *inside* truth is that the nurse, whether she knew it or not, was being Christ to Anne in her pain. As Anne says, "It *was* Christ, and it *was* the nurse."

That story, for Anne Squire, has become a myth because it has a meaning far deeper than facts. "Whenever I have felt alone, that experience comes back to me. It affirmed for me that I wasn't alone, that God was always there with me." (From an interview by Jim Taylor, *The United Church Observer*, January 1995.)

Many of us remember and were part of the black liberation movement in the U.S.A. during the '60s. Since that time, Rev. Martin Luther King Jr. has become something of a mythological figure. The President has declared a Martin Luther King Jr. day each January. Children learn his story in the schools. That story has become a myth, because it is deeply meaningful for many people. The story of Dr. King and the black liberation movement is history. I was there. But it is also myth because the story has such deep meaning for Americans generally and for African-Americans particularly.

Some myths are historical fact. Some are fiction. Most are a mixture of both.

So much to think about, so little to believe in

As a society and a church, we have grown away from mythology as a way of knowing. Myths are hard to categorize and impossible to control. The industrial and the scientific eras have sprayed the garden of our souls with the herbicide of logic and analysis. The rich mythology and tradition that carried the beauty and the baseness of our heritage has been sanitized and plasticized. Children don't hear stories from their elders any longer. They are not given spiritual food – they are given a carefully tested recipe describing food. In their hunger they watch TV, which offers spiritual junk food. And the children die of spiritual malnutrition.

What, after all, is Holy Scripture? What makes that motley collection of writings worthy of the name Holy Bible? In a way we only dimly understand God was part of the creation of those writings, and so those writings help us to sense at a deep and profound level who we are and what our lives mean.

The Bible is holy because God was there, not worried the slightest about technicalities of history or science or theology, but sitting at the campfires of the wandering Arameans, infecting their conversation with love and insight, asking holy questions through the arguments of the rabbis, nudging the early church to notice the cosmic Christ as they wrote their memories of the historical Jesus.

The Bible records the Christian myth. Even if someone argued that *none* of it ever occurred, I would *still* claim the Bible is the vessel of profound, life-giving, and holy truth.

We lay people have lost the Bible, the richest source of our Christian mythology. The right wing of the church has embalmed the biblical story in its desperate attempt to keep it unchanging and totally dependable. The left wing of the church has dissected the scriptural myth, taken it out of the hands of the people, and reserved it for the scholars and through them for the priests. And we, the lay people, have not tried very hard to take it back. Scholars, offering hypotheses on what Jesus certainly said or certainly did not say, distract us from the mythological truths injected by writers and editors and copyists. We, the people of the church, the so-called living body of Christ, have been left without myth or metaphor to give flesh to our faith. We are given so much to think about, but so little to believe in.

It's time we learned from the unlettered folk who gathered in remote *barrios* to read the stories for themselves and to marinate those stories in the broth of their own culture and circumstances. They fell in love with the myth and become part of it. That myth gave them power to analyze and to act. In much the same way, black, native, feminist, and homosexual groups have sometimes grabbed the raw biblical myth and made it their own. Each, in different places and in different ways, found their own story and were empowered. They had a myth that gave them meaning. That myth gave them power to understand and to do, and often, then, to go back to the biblical account to study it historically for additional insight.

We in the liberal church have embraced a gospel of analytical rationality. But analytical rationality will not help us find our lost buttons even though the light it provides is good. Neither will its opposite, irrational anarchy, which provides no light at all. And we will be a powerless church until we find our buttons again.

It's not that this rational approach is wrong. It's just that it tends to squeeze all the juice out of the gospel. It's a dry crust rather than a loaf of steaming, aromatic fresh bread.

Walter Brueggemann calls it a "reduced" truth, a reductionism that offers a stone when we are hungering for bread. Brueggemann quotes Walt Whitman (*Leaves of Grass*) who says that after the best logical, scientific, and neatly organized minds have done their best,

> Finally shall come the poet worthy of that name,
> The true son of God shall come singing his songs.

So reclaim your Bible. It's God's gift to you. And remember, before you do anything else with it, enjoy it – love the stories and sing the songs.

There's lots to learn in the Bible. But let that wait. First... *first, you fall in love.*

God, Eve and Adam
from dust, to the breath of life

Introduction

From way beyond the mists of history come two stories about how things began. They are both at the beginning of the Bible in a book called Genesis, which means, "beginnings." The two stories are very different.

The first creation story ends at Genesis 2:3, and the second one begins one sentence later. The first has the mystery of a metaphysical explanation – the second has the pungent richness of an ancient myth. Sometimes people try to reconcile the two. It doesn't work. Instead, enjoy the stories for the wisdom they offer.

I like the second story better because it resonates with life. Not many artists have painted pictures of the first creation myth, but they've had a field day with the second because it has people, conflict, sex, intrigue, a villain we can hate – everything you need in a good story. But unlike a Harlequin romance or a TV soap, this story struggles with profound questions: What is the meaning of sex? Why do we have to die? Why do we have to work hard? Why does living hurt so much sometimes? And the most profound question of all: How is it that questions of good and evil don't bother the animals at all, but humans are constantly fussing with them?

Like all good myths, this story is true "on the inside." It offers no answers, but lots of insights.

The story in the Bible – *paraphrase of Genesis 2:4b–3:24*

When God made the earth and heaven, there were no plants in the field, and no herbs, because God hadn't made it rain as yet. And there was nobody to cultivate the soil. But there was a stream rising from the ground and it watered the whole earth.

Then God formed a human being from the dust of the ground, and breathed into the human's nostrils the breath of life. And the human became a living soul.

God planted a garden in the area called Eden, in the east, and there God put the human. Out of the garden God grew every pleasant-looking fruit tree. The tree of life is also there in the middle of the garden, and the tree of the knowledge of good and evil.

A river flows out of Eden and it waters the garden, and then it divides and becomes four branches.

God put the human into the Garden of Eden to cultivate it and to take care of it. "You can eat anything from any of the trees," God said, "but not from the tree of the knowledge of good and evil. If you eat that, you will die."

Then God said, "It's not good that this human live alone. I will make a companion for the human. So God created animals and birds out of the ground, and each one was brought to the human to be named, and whatever the human called it, that's what it was called. The human named all the cattle and birds, but there was still no one that could really be a partner to the human.

So God caused a deep sleep to fall on the human, and then God took the side of the human, and closed up the place from which it was taken. God made a woman and brought her to the man. Then the man said,

Finally, this is bone of my bone,

flesh of my flesh,

This one shall be called Woman

For she was taken out of Man.

That is why a man leaves his father and his mother, and joins with his wife. They become one flesh.

The two of them were naked, but they were not embarrassed.

Now the snake was more clever than any of the other animals God had made. The snake said to the woman, "Did God really say, 'You can eat from any tree in the garden?'"

"We're allowed to eat any of the fruit, except God told us not to eat the fruit of the tree in the middle of the garden. 'Don't even touch it,' God said, 'or you will die.'"

"You won't die! God knows that when you eat that fruit, you will be wise and be like God. You will know the difference between good and evil."

So when the woman saw that the fruit was good for food, that it was good looking fruit, and that it would make her wise, she picked some of it. She ate it, and gave some to her husband.

Then suddenly they realized they were both naked. So they sewed themselves some loincloths from fig leaves.

They heard the sound of God walking in the garden in the cool of the evening. And the man and his wife hid themselves among the trees. God called to them, "Where are you?"

"I heard you walking in the Garden," said the man, "and I hid myself because I was naked."

"Who said you were naked? Have you eaten from the forbidden tree?"

"Well, the woman you gave me, well, she gave the fruit to me so I ate it."

"What have you done?" God asked the woman.

"It was the serpent who tricked me, so I ate."

"Because you have done this, you will all be cursed," said God. "The snake will crawl on its belly. The woman will have pain in childbearing. The man will have to earn his food by working and sweating, and in the end, you shall all die. You are made of dust. You will return to dust."

The man gave his wife a name – Eve, which means, "the mother of all living things." And God made them clothing out of the skins of animals.

"Because these humans have become like us," God said, "and they know the difference between good and evil, there is a danger that they might also eat from the tree of life and live forever." So God expelled them from the garden of Eden to work the ground from which they came.

Then, at the east of the garden of Eden, God stationed an angel with a flaming sword to guard the way to the tree of life.

Why I wrote this story

I don't remember why. I do know where the basic idea came from. Rabbi Harold Kushner, in his book *When Bad Things Happen to Good People,* explains a little difficulty many folks have had with Genesis 1:26, in the first creation myth, where God says, "let us create humans in *our* image." Why the plural when there is only one God?

The simple answer is that, at one time, the Hebrews believed in several gods. But Kushner has a better idea, I think. He says God was talking to the animals which were created in verse 26, and saying, "Okay, animals, let us create a human that is like you animals, and like me, God."

I liked that. I am both a "naked ape" *and* made in "God's image." Kushner's idea got my imagination percolating.

I also had something bouncing around in my head about a God who loves to create and who loves creation. On the negative side, some of the sexism in the second creation story is a bit hard to swallow. I think that's why I may have written this semi-biblical fantasy.

I've read this to dozens of audiences and hundreds of people. Sometimes I ask people to hear the story from a particular perspective. I invite the young women to listen from Eve's point of view, the young men to listen from Adam's perspective. Then I suggest that older people listen as God, and all the middle-aged folks get to be the snake. Then we talk about it. It's great fun.

An important note: Some of my homosexual friends have wondered why they are not included in my creation fantasy. Parts of the story are an unabashed celebration of heterosexuality, and homosexual persons sometimes feel left out.

I'm sorry that is so. Every story is exclusive in some sense. Every story is only a tiny spotlight on a small part of the human experience. This whole book is about getting people to imagine their own mythology—stories that touch on many varieties of experience. A story is complete only for the person who dreamed it.

The story invites you to ask the holy question, "What if..." and then to tell many more stories about many more acts of creation.

"What if..."

Way back when, at the very beginning of things, there was a God with an unpronounceable name. Something like "Yahweh." Probably close, but nobody was sure.

Now this Yahweh, being after all, well, God, shouldn't have *needed* anything. But this God was the *only* God and therefore all alone. And, well, Yahweh was lonely. So Yahweh started making things. And in each little creation, Yahweh invested love. Deep love.

Yahweh loved making things. Round things like worlds and growing things like dandelions and creeping things like worms. And things that walked and ran. It was fun too. Yahweh raced with the gazelle, and of course won hands down because Yahweh was God and therefore the best at everything. And Yahweh made faces at the chimp and the chimp really broke up laughing because God could make funnier faces than anyone. But the gazelles and the chimps and all the other animals were mostly concerned with necessary things like eating and copulating and bearing offspring.

In those days, the animals could talk. And Yahweh had interesting conversations with them. Interesting, and sometimes frustrating. There were two words the animals never used. "What if..." Yahweh used those two words constantly.

"What if, instead of having babies come out of eggs, we grew them inside their mother's womb?"

None of the animals could understand that. "I laid a 200-pound egg last week," said the elephant. "I was going for a record, and now you decide to change it."

"What if you had a 300-pound baby instead?" Yahweh asked. "Then it'd be ready to go. You wouldn't have to sit on it for 16 months."

"I suppose. But we never did it that way before," said the elephant.

The birds and the insects and reptiles seemed to be the most conservative of all. "No way, José!" said the blue jay. "I like sitting on eggs. I like it! I like it!"

"So all right already!" said Yahweh. "What if birds, insects, and reptiles did eggs, and the rest of you had the new, improved ready-to-go kid?"

"What if...What if..." said the baboon. "Can't you leave things alone instead of creating all the time?"

"No, I can't. That's who I am," said Yahweh. "You're a survivor. I'm a creator. And oh, how I'd like someone to create with me."

"Here we go again," said the dinosaur.

"What if..." Yahweh said kind of introspectively... "What if I made something that's a little like both of us? What if we called it a 'human'?"

Yahweh God was silent for awhile. Then, "Let us make a human in our image. A being that's going to be like you animals in all kinds of ways. An animal that can run like the gazelle and make stupid faces like the chip... a being that will be preoccupied with necessary things like eating and copulating and bearing young and staying alive..."

Yahweh paused for a moment. "But this being, this human, will be like me too. This human will know what it's like to be God. This human will understand the difference between good and evil. This human will get the point of a joke. This human will understand the words, 'what if...'"

So Yahweh God went to work. Yahweh took some of the dust of the ground, moistened it with the water of life, and shaped it into a beautiful creature called "human." Then Yahweh held the new being close, like a mother cradling her baby, and gently breathed the breath of life into this new creation. And the human – the human became a living soul!

The animals gasped. The human was beautiful. Just beautiful. Yahweh looked and smiled at the human. "Behold," Yahweh said, "this is *very* good."

Yahweh and the human had a wonderful time together. Yahweh and the human loved to begin sentences with "What if..." But some of the animals were much more logical than God. They pointed out a small flaw in the divine plan.

"Ah, God," said the orangutan. "You said this human was going to be like us animals...preoccupied with necessary things like eating and copulating. The eating part is no problem. The human manages to eat alone, all right. But if you have a copulator, you also have to have a copulatee."

"Good point," said God. "But I'll go you one better. This human is created in my image. The human is like me in the most important way possible. So this human will need more than just another human to copulate with and to bear offspring with."

So God caused a deep sleep to fall on the first human, and from the side of the one, made another – another human, very much like the first but different in just the right ways.

"Look!" God said to the animals. "These humans can do far more than copulate. Whenever humans bring their bodies together in care and tenderness, they will know that one was taken from the other, and that one is incomplete without the other. They will know each other in love, and it will be a sacrament. A divine and holy sacrament.

"And these humans, out of their lovemaking, and because they will know sacredness in their loving, they will be able to create the world *with* me."

Then the great God Yahweh looked at the two humans standing there, bare naked and beautiful. And God loved them and gave them names. Eve and Adam. And Yahweh smiled a smile as wide as the rainbow.

Yahweh enjoyed creating with the humans...enjoyed the long "what if..." conversations they had strolling through the gardens. But Yahweh also was just a little worried. The humans were getting a little careless about their creating. It was just too easy for them to say, "what if..." and ZAP, there it was. Then Yahweh knew these humans were incomplete. Something was missing. It was fun creating with these humans, but they seemed so... God wasn't sure what. The garden was perfect. Everyone was having fun. But it didn't seem to mean anything.

Suddenly God asked a whole new question. The question was "Why?"

God asked the humans. "I have a new question. It's even bigger than 'what if.' The question is 'why?'"

"I don't get it," said Adam.

"Why? What do you mean, 'why?'" asked Eve.

There was a long, long pause.

Finally God said, "What if..."

"What if what?" asked Eve.

God was silent for a long while.

"Look, Eve, Adam. That tree over there. You can't eat any of the fruit off it, see. That's reserved for me. Touch it, and I'll stomp on you good. Y'hear?"

"Whatever you say," shrugged Adam.

"But why?" Eve wanted to know, surprised that she was asking God's new question.

"Precisely!" roared God. "Now do as you're told."

But Eve wondered. She almost thought she heard a challenge in Yahweh's order. Adam shrugged and walked off, but Eve sat down, looked at the tree, her eyes sparkling with the new challenge.

Eve made up a tall tale about a serpent tempting her (just in case God should catch her red-handed), and then after dark one night, she snitched some of the fruit from the forbidden tree. And she slipped a few pieces into the salad Adam was making for supper. He never knew the difference.

Yahweh of course, knew the difference. After all, Yahweh was God. God knew everything.

"All right," God said. "Everybody out of the pool. You didn't play by the rules. You tried to think for yourselves. You tried to act on your own. So the party's over. Out!"

God sounded furious. But Eve thought she saw the hint of a smile in God's eyes. Or was it perhaps that God was shedding a divine tear? Yahweh was both mother and father of this race of humans. Yahweh had enjoyed their childlike innocence, and it seemed like a shame for them to have to grow up so quickly. It was both a tear and a smile. Yahweh, like all parents, felt both joy and pain watching the kids go off into the world.

So God put heavenly arms around the couple and gave them a hug. "You're going to have to work for your food," God said to them somewhat sadly. "But the work will build strength. Work will put you in touch with the earth from which you were formed.

"And you are going to know pain and danger and anger and alienation and shame. And heartbreak."

Eve and Adam could feel that great heavenly body quake. God was crying.

"I'm sorry it has to be this way," Yahweh said to them very softly. "But if you don't know about pain and danger and alienation and shame, you'll never know about joy and comfort and love and community and ecstasy.

"And death too. You've got to die so that you can live."

"But why?" Eve asked.

"You will never understand," said Yahweh, "but if you remember how we created this world together, and how much I love you, then sometimes, just for an instant, you will know."

So Adam and Eve went off to start the human race. And Yahweh grinned and cried at their naked buttocks bouncing away from paradise and into the world.

"Be fruitful and multiply," God said. "Fill the earth. You're in charge of it. Be gentle with our creation."

As the couple turned for one final wave, God called out, "Don't forget to call home. Often! Please."

Sarah
joy in her old age

Introduction

Sarah's name means "princess," though she spent very little, if any, time inside a palace. Her story (or legend) dates from the 18th century, BCE, when she and her husband Abraham left Ur of the Chaldeans to go to Haran and then to Canaan, with various side trips.

Sarah's great beauty was a source of considerable pain for her. Twice, according to the story, Abraham passed her off as his sister, and she was taken into a harem – once in Egypt and another time near Gaza. She *was* Abraham's half-sister, which is a pretty slim excuse.

Sarah spent most of her life yearning for a baby, and listening to God promising children to her. Indeed, God kept promising to make a great nation out of Abraham's and Sarah's descendants. But nothing happened. Sarah gave up hope and told Abraham to have sex with her servant Hagar, so that Hagar would bear a child for them. Then, when Sarah was past 90, she and Abraham had a visit from two strangers who were angels, or God, or...? But they *did* promise Sarah a baby. When it finally arrived, she named him Isaac, which means "laughter."

Be sure to read the next story too, the one about Hagar. Because Sarah's good news meant that Hagar lost everything.

The story in the Bible – *paraphrase of Genesis 18:9–15*

The two strangers said to Abraham, "Where is Sarah, your wife?"

"She's there, in the tent."

Then one of the strangers said, "I will come back here before long, and when I do, I'm telling you for sure, Sarah will have given birth to a son."

Sarah was listening at the entrance to the tent, just behind him. Now Sarah and Abraham were both old. In fact, Sarah was already past her menopause. So Sarah laughed to herself. "I am old and my husband is old! Am I still to know pleasure?"

Then one of the strangers, an angel representing God, asked, "Why did Sarah laugh, and wonder if she could have a child now that she is old. Is anything too wonderful for God. I tell you, I will come back in due season, and when I do, Sarah will have a son."

"I didn't laugh," said Sarah.

"Oh yes you did," said the angel.

Why I wrote this story

Madeleine L'Engle, the noted author of *A Wrinkle In Time* and many other exceptional books, was holding a seminar at the Vancouver School of Theology. (She too is fascinated by the richness and the insight we gain when we follow our imaginations into these biblical stories and allow them to speak to us.)

Authors often use the birth metaphor to describe the writing experience. During the seminar, Madeleine was imagining her way into the story of King David and the various women in his life, a novel that was later published as *Certain Women* (HarperSanFrancisco, 1992). Here was an older woman giving birth to a book, a process she described sometimes with pain, sometimes with laughter. Madeleine seemed very much like Sarah to me.

Certain Women is about the death of a famous actor named David, who is modeled after King David in the Bible. The women in the story bear the names and personalities of the women in King David's life. I believe that living herself into the story of King David and his death made it possible for Madeleine to write her next book, *A Two Part Invention*, the story of her marriage and of the death of her husband, also a well-known actor.

In our seminar, Madeleine invited us to write the story behind the biblical story. I was always fascinated by the story of aged Sarah laughing at the angel's preposterous pronouncement. Now I had a "model" for my Sarah, and this poem is the result.

"To proclaim a dancing God"

At first it was a cough;
then a stifled gasp;
then a watering of nose and eyes –
a rasping, wheezing, rattling noise
that might have been a full-blown case of asthma.
Or a stroke.
But it was laughter.
It was laughter!
From arthritic toes to gray and thinning hair,
it was a laughter from despair to hope –
laughter from the tomb to resurrection.

The old crone pulled the tent flap tight across her toothless
mouth
to hide her laughter;
Hide it from her sniggering, impotent mate –
Hide the laughter from the bright-eyed strangers
who came
announcing new and ancient promises,
a child of hope
for Sarah's ancient, arid womb –
for Abraham's ancient, arid land.

But hide it from the future, she could not.
Sarah birthed a promise,
in a child named Laughter,
And so proclaimed a dancing God
into the ages.

Hagar
who survived a sentence of death

Introduction

Hagar's story is one of the most poignant in the Hebrew scriptures. As a female slave, she was totally at the mercy of her owners, Abraham and Sarah.

As Sarah got older, she became convinced she would never have a child. So she told her husband to go to Hagar, her Egyptian slave, and have a baby with her. That was considered quite acceptable at the time. Hagar, of course, had no say in the matter.

A child named Ishmael was born to Hagar. A few years later, Sarah herself had a child, and immediately the question hung over them all. Who would inherit the family name or blessing, and who would inherit the family wealth? Sarah forced Abraham to throw Hagar and her son out into the desert, which was equivalent to a sentence of death.

Hagar and Ishmael are regarded by the Arabs as their ancestors. There is a legend that both of them are buried in the sacred *Kaaba* in Mecca.

The story in the Bible – *paraphrase of Genesis 21:8–21*

Isaac, the child of Abraham and Sarah began to grow. He was weaned, which was the occasion for a big feast.

But one day, Sarah saw Ishmael, the son of Hagar the Egyptian and Abraham, playing with her son Isaac.

Sarah said to Abraham. "Throw this slave woman out. I don't want her son to share the inheritance along with my son Isaac."

Abraham was very upset by that request, because he loved Ishmael too. But God said to Abraham, "Don't worry about Ishmael and about the slave woman. Do whatever Sarah asks. It is through Isaac that I will make a nation of your offspring that will be named for you. As for Ishmael, I'll do the same for him. Because he is your child, I'll make a nation from his offspring also."

So Abraham got up early in the morning, took some bread and a skin of water and gave it to Hagar. Then he put the child Ishmael on her shoulder and sent her away.

Hagar wandered around in the wilderness of Beersheba till the water was all gone. Then she put the child down under a bush, and went and sat some distance away because she was thinking, "I can't watch my own child die." Then she broke down and wept in anguish.

God heard the voice of the boy. And an angel called to Hagar from heaven. "Why are you crying, Hagar? Don't be afraid, because God has heard the boy crying as he lies there. Go, pick up the child and hold him close. His descendants will be a great nation."

Then God helped Hagar to see a well of water nearby. She went and filled up the skin of water and gave her son a drink.

So God was with the boy as he grew up. Ishmael lived in the desert, and became very skilled in the use of the bow. He lived in the wilderness of Paran, and Hagar got a wife for him from Egypt.

Why I wrote this story

I wrote this story out of guilt. At the Madeleine L'Engle seminar, at which I wrote the preceding story about Sarah, Madeleine asked us, "Who else is in the story?" Bev (my spouse) responded immediately. "Hagar," she said. "Hagar is out in the cold."

After I wrote the collection of children's Bible stories *Living God's Way**, one of the reviewers pointed out that I had left out the story of Hagar and her baby.

I suppose I resisted writing the story. Then, as I got started, I began to feel her despair, her terror, the anger of her experience. I realized Hagar must have been an exceptionally strong person to survive such an ordeal. The face of Hagar became the face I saw in a church magazine – an article about a woman from Nicaragua. Her husband and a son had been killed by soldiers. At her breast was a new baby. The father of that child was a soldier. She had been raped.

I don't remember her name, nor even the magazine where I read the article. But I do remember the eyes of this Nicaraguan Hagar. Her eyes blazed with anger and purpose, while her arms held her baby with tenderness and love.

---

* *Living God's Way* was later published as *The Family Story Bible* and included the story of Hagar.

It is that face, those eyes that I saw, when I wrote the story of Hagar.

"Is this your idea of a good time, God?"

She sat on a small rock in the blazing sun, rocking back and forth, back and forth, clutching her arms about herself, trying not to hear the distant wail of her son, her dying son. A body-wracking sob shuddered through her, and then a cry, and then a scream of terror and anger directed at anything, everything, directed at God, though Hagar knew that God was nowhere near.

The wail of her son stopped. He would die soon, then she would die, and it would be all over. Then out from nowhere that she knew, came another scream, a screech – a cry of anger, of defiance, perhaps of hate. Hate at God? Why not? What had God done for her except lead her into hope, then throw her out into the unforgiving desert with her son to die.

They say your whole life plays before you, just before you die. You see it all in panorama, all the good and bad of it, all the hope and hate of it. And Hagar saw the child she was, taken from a home she later learned was Egypt, sold as slave to Sarah on whom she waited hand and foot for years and years. Old Sarah. Barren Sarah. Sarah without child, who argued and cajoled at God to give her children.

Just 14 years ago Sarah grabbed her slave girl's arm, pushed her roughly into her tent and said to her husband Abraham. "Here. Take this girl. Make her pregnant. If I can't bear a child for you, she can. But it will be *my* child. Do you hear that, slave?" Hagar nodded. She had no choice.

Hagar bore the child as she was told. She nursed the boy. She loved the boy. But Sarah made it clear. "That's not your child."

And Hagar should have known. Slaves don't taunt their owners. But her contempt of Sarah grew faster than the child within her belly. "You're right," she snarled at Sarah. "He's *your* child, O barren one."

And Sarah lashed right back in anger. Abused and battered, Hagar fled into the desert. It didn't seem as bad that time. Hagar felt the love of God inside her then, and when she prayed, she seemed to feel an answer. "Give Sarah a bit of time to cool down, and then go back," God said. "You will bear your child. Give him the name of Ishmael, which means, God hears. God will hear you, Hagar. Your child shall grow up strong, and you shall hold his children on your knee. You and Ishmael will be the forebears of a kind and gentle people."

Hagar tried not to show the young son Ishmael to the angry matriarch. And for awhile it worked.

Then one day the rumors flew around the tribe – rumors of angels visiting, rumors of Sarah and of Abraham laughing loud and long at the ludicrous good news that Sarah would bear a son.

"Great news," thought Hagar. "Great news for everyone, but not for me and not for my son Ishmael," now grown into his early teens. While joy and promise sang from every tent as Sarah birthed a son named Isaac, a son named Laughter, Hagar did not laugh. A sense of deep foreboding filled her soul.

The toddler Isaac wandered happily from tent to tent, and Ishmael was a kind and gentle lad who saw the baby fall and hurt his knee a little, who picked him up to comfort him. When Sarah walked around the tent, she saw Ishmael with her Isaac, and screamed and cried and once again told Hagar to "Get out! I don't want to ever set eyes on you again. Get out!"

"But Sarah," Abraham tried to say, "It was you who brought Hagar to me. It was you who said that we should have a child through her. And now you want to throw them out? It isn't right!"

"That bastard boy of yours is old enough to take your place, old man," Sarah hissed. "If you die, he could inherit everything, and your son Isaac, the child God sent to us, would be out on his ear. So get rid of her and the boy now. Right now."

Abraham talked to God. "If I send Hagar and Ishmael out into the desert they will die," he said. "What should I do?"

"Send them," God replied. "I'll work it out."

"Sure, God, you'll work it out!" Hagar screamed at the blazing, copper sky. "Can you see my son over there. He's quiet now. Maybe he's dead already. He's lying by that bush. I couldn't bear to watch him die. Abraham sent us out here; he sent his own son out here with one lousy skin of water. Hardly any food. Well, we always do as we're told, God. You want us to come out here and die, we come out here and die. Is this your idea of a good time, God?"

"Go and hold the boy," a voice within her seemed to say. "Go and put your arms around the boy."

Hagar stumbled over rocks and thorns to take the long thin body of her son into her arms. She could not tell if Ishmael was still alive. She poured her mother love into the boy, and cried her tears, and through them saw, not far from where she sat, a well. Through the water of her tears she saw a well. Water.

She almost dropped the boy in her hurry to fill the skin with water, then to press it to the thin cracked lips of Ishmael, who at first responded not at all. But then there was some movement, and slowly bit by bit he drank, and Hagar's hopes renewed.

Hagar's hopes renewed, then crashed once more as she remembered who she was, a slave, and where she was. Nowhere.

Again she cried, she looked toward the well, and from the deepest well within her soul she heard a voice. "From you and Ishmael shall come a people," said the voice of God within her. "You will survive. Your son will grow. And he shall have a wife and you shall be grandmother to a fine and gentle race of people; a race of people who will know the pain that you have known; a race of people who will stand weeping outside the tents of wealthy men."

"You shall live, my child," she whispered to the son she held so close to her. "You shall live, my Ishmael, and you shall grow, and you and I shall be the forebears of a fine and gentle race of people." And then she added in a firm and hopeful voice: "A race of people who will suffer and survive."

Then Hagar drank some water for herself. She drank it deep, and knew that even though it would not be through Abraham and Sarah and their race, Hagar and her son Ishmael were loved of God, and children of the promise.

Abraham
a passionate man who talked with God

Introduction

The saga of Abraham and Sarah is full of drama, and no part of the story is more painful than Abraham's near sacrifice of Isaac. When I wrote a children's version of that story for the book *The Family Story Bible*, I went through many drafts because I was concerned that children reading it might see a justification of child abuse. That danger is there for adults as well. "God said..." can be the introduction to an act of terror.

Abraham, whose name means "father is exalted," begins the saga for the Hebrew people. He is the first of the great patriarchs, who set out with his beautiful wife Sarah from a land called Ur because he felt he was called by God. He and the semi-reluctant Sarah wander from one place to another, always following God's call and God's promise to make them a great nation. Abraham is determined to obey his desert God who seems downright capricious at times. But his passion and impulsiveness keep Abraham moving, while his deep desire to be obedient and faithful keep him, more or less, on track.

God keeps promising this couple that they will have children, that they will become a great nation. Their descendants will be as many as the stars. But nothing happens and Sarah does not have a child till she is past 90. Then, God tells Abraham to make a human sacrifice out of that child, Isaac.

It is hard to be faithful when the God you believe implicitly tells you to destroy the one you love most dearly.

The story in the Bible – *a paraphrase of Genesis 22:1–18*
In those days, God tempted Abraham. God said, "Abraham."

"I'm here."

"Take your son, your only son Isaac whom you love, and go to the land of Moriah, and offer him there as a burnt offering on one of the mountains which I will show you."

So Abraham got up early in the morning, saddled his mule, and took two of his young servants with him, as well as his son Isaac. He also took the wood for the burnt offering and went toward the place God had told him. On the third day, Abraham looked up and saw the place in the distance.

Then Abraham said to the two young servants, "Stay here with the mule. I and the lad will go over there and worship, and then we will come back to you."

Abraham took the wood for the burnt offering and put it on his son Isaac, while he carried the fire and the knife, and both of them went together.

"Father," Isaac said, "We have the fire and the wood. But where is the lamb for the burnt offering?"

"God will provide a lamb for a burnt offering."

When they came to the place God had told Abraham about, he built an altar, then he put the wood on it, and he tied up his son and laid him on it. Then Abraham raised his hand with the knife to kill his son.

But an angel of God called to him from heaven. "Abraham! Abraham! Don't touch the lad. Don't hurt him. For now I know that you fear God, since you didn't withhold your only son from me."

Then Abraham looked up and saw a ram caught by its horns in the bushes. Abraham took the ram, and used it for the burnt offering instead of his son. Abraham named that place, "God Will Provide." To this day, people say, "On the mountain, God will provide."

Then the Angel of God called out of heaven a second time. "I have made a promise," said God, "that because you did this – you did not withhold your only son – I will bless you and multiply your children as the stars in heaven, and as the sand on the sea, and they shall conquer all their enemies. And in your descendants, all the nations of the earth will be blessed because you obeyed my voice."

Why I wrote this story

Few stage and film performances have impressed me as much as *Fiddler on the Roof*. It was a good story with fine music and it connected with some of my family's history.

What moves me most about *Fiddler* is the character of Tevya, especially as it was interpreted by the actor Topol. That personality was right out of the patriarchs in the Hebrew Bible. They were passionate men who talked with God as they would talk with a good and treasured friend. There were times they called that friend to account. And running through their lives and their dialog with God was a fundamental sense of humor – a visceral appreciation of the divine ludicrousness of it all.

Old Tevya quotes scripture at God, then laughs at himself. He chides God for making him poor. "Would it spoil some vast eternal plan / If I were a wealthy man?" And when Tevya and Golda find themselves leaving home to move to a strange and foreign land, their God travels with them.

Tevya talked not only to God, but to his family and friends and his Rabbi – especially to Golda to whom he had been married 25 years. In other words, God and Tevya talked to each other directly, but the meanings of those conversations were focused within the worshiping community.

Talking directly to God is a dangerous business. The only protection we have is our community. Tevya has his synagogue. I have my church. The only way to prevent the destruction of people by "divine word" is to have that "word from God" discussed with others in our community of faith.

As I imagined my way into this story, Abraham began to look and sound like Tevya. They both had a conversational relationship to God. They both had strong wives who were not afraid to question that "word from God." I wonder if Abraham would have heard God's word about killing Isaac somewhat differently if he'd talked to Sarah about it.

I wonder if the angel who spoke to him and pointed out the ram in the bush sounded just a little bit like Sarah.

"On the other hand..."

God, you never said it would be easy.

You promised Sarah and me a new land to live in. You promised we'd be the forebears of a great people. And it all takes time, I know, I know. And you sent us Isaac – oh what a son he is, God, what a son he is; fine boy, my Isaac.

And you said it was through Isaac that Sarah and me would be the ancestors of a race of people. "Look at the stars," you said. Do you remember you said that. Of course you remember.

So I looked at the stars, but I can't count that far. Still, that would be a lot of folks, God. Can you handle that many? I mean, just with Sarah and me and our little tribe, you've had your hands full, right? If you make as many people as there are stars, can you pay attention to them all?

Or are you going to be a little easier on them? Because it's not an easy thing, you know, God. Maybe you don't understand how tough it is. You're God, so for you such things are easy. I'm just a human being. You made me out of dust, remember. Aren't you expecting just a bit much from a walking lump of dust, God?

All right, I know. You've always delivered on your promises. Well, except for that promise about as many people as there are stars. I guess I won't be around to see that.

But God, why this? It makes no sense – no sense at all. It made sense when you told me to pack up and leave home and go to a country that you'd show us. Fine, I can understand that.

And granted, we had to wait a long time before you delivered on the child you promised. Such a child. Oy! A beautiful boy, with his mother's dark eyes. And they say he has my nose. A good nose for a man. And we laughed when we heard he was coming, oh Sarah and me we laughed so hard. And so we named the boy Isaac, which means 'laughter.'" Did you know that, God? Of course you know.

So now, why this? Why this? On the one hand, you told us we would become a great nation through Isaac. On the other hand, here I am walking up the mountainside with my son Isaac beside me, under your orders to make a sacrifice of him. You have told me to put my own son on an altar and to kill him there as a sacrifice to you.

"If you really love me, you will do it." I heard you say that, God. You came through loud and clear. "Take the boy up the mountain and make a human sacrifice out of him." I know, I know, that's what you said.

But he's my boy, God. Have you any idea what it might be like to watch your own child die? Especially when he's innocent. He hasn't done anything wrong. I've done wrong. I mean, you know how often I've messed up. So is my son going to die for my sins?

Yes, I believe you God. I trust you. But I don't understand. And I wonder if you understand what it's like to be a parent. Maybe you should try it sometime, God. Then you might know what it was like to love a child more than anything in the world, and then to have your child taken from you.

All right, already. I'm sorry. You're God. You know what you are doing. You told me to sacrifice my son and so here I am.

"Isaac, my son. I love you with my whole life. I know you will not understand what I am going to do. I don't understand it myself. I only know that God has told me I must do this, and so I must. God has a plan. I have no idea what it is, but I know that God has a plan and that somehow all these things work together for good, if we believe.

"Please don't look at me with those big, dark Sarah eyes. Close your eyes, and know that God loves you and that I love you. Trust, my son."

So this is the moment, God. It has come down to this moment. This is the test, and I will meet it. But if I am wrong, if it is not your voice, God, that I heard, please be merciful and take my life.

One deep breath, one deep breath to breathe your strength into my soul, and then, O God, it will be done. One deep breath and...

A ram. A ram bleating there in the bush. A ram. God be praised, a ram, an offering in place of Isaac. Thank you, God.

Yes, of course, I understand. You test us God, and if we are faithful, you provide. You ask of us our lives, our total faithful lives, and promise us the hope, the beauty, and the truth. You walk us into death, and offer us the resurrection.

Rebecca
an outstanding matriarch

Introduction

When Abraham and Sarah moved to Canaan, they left behind some relatives in what is now northern Syria, and that's where Abraham turned when he wanted a wife for Isaac. Sarah had died. She had been a strong woman and her death must have left a large void in their lives.

There are indications throughout the story that Isaac was somewhat of a "mama's boy." This is not too surprising since he was Sarah's only child, born to her in old age, and one whom Abraham almost killed as a human sacrifice.

So Abraham loaded a servant with expensive gifts and in effect said, "Go to my home town and buy Isaac a nice wife."

What he had in mind was probably an obedient and hard-working girl who would have lots of baby boys. What he got was Rebecca, who is one of the outstanding matriarchs of the Bible.

The story in the Bible – *a paraphrase of Genesis 24:10–67*

The servant took ten of Abraham's camels and went. He took all kinds of expensive gifts from Abraham, and went to the city of Nahor. Outside the city, near the well, he made his camels kneel down. It was near evening, the time when the women usually came out to get water.

So the servant said a prayer. "O God of my master Abraham. Please help me be successful today, and in so doing show your love for my master Abraham. I'm standing here at the well, and all the young women are coming to get water. I will say to one of them, 'Please give me a drink of water.' And if she then says, 'Of course. And then I will also water your camels,' let her be the one you have chosen for Isaac. If you do this, I'll know that you really love my master."

While he was still praying, he looked up and there was Rebecca. She was in fact a relative of Abraham. Rebecca had a water jar on her shoulder. She was beautiful and a virgin.

Rebecca went down to the bottom of the well, filled her jar and came up. Then the servant ran up to her and said, "Excuse me. Please let me have just a tiny drink from your jar."

"Of course, sir," she said and took her jar off her shoulder and gave him a drink. "Would you like me to also get water for your camels?" So Rebecca drew water for all his camels. Meanwhile, the servant looked at her in silence, wondering if she was in fact the one he should choose as a bride for Isaac.

When the camels had finished, the servant took a gold nose ring and two bracelets for her arms and gave them to her. Then he said, "Tell me who your father is. Is there room in your father's house for me to spend the night?"

"My father's name is Bethuel," Rebecca said. "We have lots of straw and lots of food for the camels, and a place for you to spend the night."

"Thanks be to God," said the man. "May the God of Abraham be blessed. God has shown love to Abraham because I have been led to the home of one of his relatives."

Rebecca ran to the house and told her mother and the whole household what had happened. Rebecca had a brother named Laban. As soon as he heard his sister's story, he ran out to the servant, who was still standing by the spring . "Come in, come in. Welcome! I've got a good spot for you and your camels."

So the servant came to their house, and Laban fed his camels and gave him water to wash with, and also for the men who were with him. Then he invited the servant to come in and eat.

"I can't eat until I've told you why I came."

"Well, tell us," said Laban.

"I am a servant of Abraham. God has blessed Abraham, and made him very wealthy. Unfortunately, his wife Sarah has died. She had a baby when she was quite old, and Abraham is concerned that this boy will marry a woman from among the Canaanites, among whom they live. So he sent me here, to his relatives, to find a wife for him.

"I admit I was worried coming here. I was afraid that the wife I selected wouldn't come with me. But an angel visited me and told me that my mission would be successful.

"So today, when I came to the spring, I asked God to point the right woman out to me – the one who would not only give me a drink, but water my camels as well. That was Rebecca. She is the one God wants for Isaac's wife. So tell me, will you agree to that?"

Laban and Bethuel looked at each other and answered, "If it's God's will, then there is nothing for us to say. Here's Rebecca. Take her. Let her be Isaac's wife."

Then the servant bowed deeply before them. He brought out jewels and silver and gold and fine clothing and gave them all to Rebecca. He gave gifts to her brother and to her mother.

Then the men had a party. They ate and drank well into the night. In the morning the servant said, "I need to go back home."

Laban and Rebecca's mother said, "Let Rebecca stay behind for ten days, and then we'll let her go."

"Please don't delay me," said the servant. "God has helped make my journey successful. Now I really want to go back home right away."

"Let's ask Rebecca," said the family. "Will you go with this man?"

"Yes. Right now."

So they sent Rebecca on her way, along with her maidservant, and with many blessings.

Now Isaac was walking in the fields one evening, when he looked up and saw the camels coming. Rebecca also saw a man walking and asked the servant, "Who is that?" When she heard it was Isaac, she covered her face with her veil.

Isaac took Rebecca into his mother Sarah's tent and they were married. So Isaac felt better, since he no longer had a mother.

Why I wrote this story

It is a good story. And Rebecca is a most interesting person.

Like many stories, it is only when you dream it, play around with the details, that the inside of the story begins to speak to you. I understood who Rebecca was when I understood what was involved in watering ten camels. My encyclopedia tells me a camel can drink as much as 30 gallons. The typical water jar carries about a gallon. To get a jar full of water, Rebecca probably had to go down 20 or more steps to the bottom of the well. That translates into 300 round trips!

Ten gallons is more usual for camels, I learned during my time in Israel. But even so, that's up and down that well 100 times, with the servant and his men standing there, watching. And camels are not cuddly, lovable beasts. They are cranky and they smell and they most certainly never say thank you.

So, either Rebecca was an obedient drudge, or she had a sense of humor. As I read the rest of her story, I became convinced it was the latter. Because life was never simple or easy for her. Rebecca not only survived – she triumphed.

"Why ten stinking camels?"

"Ten camels. I should have my head examined for saying I would water ten stinking camels!"

Rebecca was muttering to herself. She had been up and down the well for almost two hours, and the camels were still drinking.

She'd been very willing at first. Her upbringing and her own good nature had prompted her to volunteer to water this man's camels. He was a stranger in town, so when he asked Rebecca for a drink, she was glad to offer him her water jar. And then she offered to water his camels too.

Finally, the last of the camels raised its head from the water trough, gave her a disdainful look, and turned away. "Well, the same to you," Rebecca thought to herself. She had never really liked camels. They had bad tempers, they had terrible body odor, and they always looked disdainful.

The man approached her. "Thank you very much," he said. "You are very kind, and you must be very tired. Here, I have something for you."

With more gentleness than Rebecca expected, he gave her two heavy gold bracelets for her arm and a ring for her nose. "Tell me whose family you belong to. And is there room for me to stay at your house tonight?"

"My father's name is Bethuel. We have plenty of room and lots of food for *all ten* of your camels." Rebecca hadn't really meant to emphasize "all ten" that way, but she was relieved when the man chuckled.

"They are thirsty beasts, aren't they?"

"I'll run ahead and tell my mother you are coming," said Rebecca. Her tired legs found new life in her excitement as she ran down the path to her home. "Mom, Laban, everybody! We're having company. I don't know who he is but I watered all ten of his camels and then he gave me all this! Look!" The whole household came running to see Rebecca's expensive gifts. "I told him he could stay here tonight."

"Who is he?" her brother Laban demanded.

"I don't know. He didn't say. But he's got something on his mind, I can tell."

"Did he say what?" Laban looked at his sister intently.

Rebecca blushed. "No, but he watched every move I made while I watered all ten of his camels."

"Well, don't stand around. Get the house cleaned. Start cooking." Laban barked the command and rushed out of the house to find this wealthy stranger.

Rebecca often thought about that night, how it had totally changed her life. The man had come to their house, identified himself as Abraham's servant, and told the family that God wanted Rebecca to come and be wife to Abraham's son Isaac. He knew it was Rebecca God wanted because she had watered all the camels. That was a sign. When Rebecca heard that, she didn't know whether to laugh or cry. "So could maybe two or three camels have been enough sign?" she wondered.

Laban and Bethuel, her father, just shrugged. "Well, if that's what God wants, that's how it has to be." Nobody bothered to ask Rebecca how she felt about all this.

The next day she was on the way. Her family had wanted her to wait a few days, to give them all a chance to say goodbye, but Rebecca refused. "If I've got to go, I want to go now. Let's not drag this thing out."

So across the desert they went, swaying on top of those cranky, smelly camels, day after hot dreary day. Motion sickness and boredom and heat. That's mostly what Rebecca remembered about the trip. That, and a churning stomach as she wondered what this Isaac was like that God wanted her to marry. "Did I have a choice?" she wondered. No. The answer was quite clearly no. Women had very few choices. "Then, God, help me make the best of whatever is to be," she prayed.

She first saw Isaac walking across the field toward her. Rebecca got down from her camel, pulled her veil down across her face and walked toward him. Rebecca saw the embarrassment, the strain in the man's face. He obviously felt he should say something but had no idea what. So Isaac turned, and walked toward his mother's tent, and she followed in silence. There in a short little ceremony, they were married. Before they said their first words to each other.

It was a strange marriage. A strange relationship. Isaac clearly wanted Rebecca to be a replacement for his strong and active mother, Sarah, who had died a few years earlier. But Rebecca was herself and Isaac learned to love her in a dependent, small-boy kind of way. She had to watch herself. Appearances were everything, and it was important that Isaac still appear to head the household.

"God, you called me here, right?" Like other desert folk, Rebecca was candid and direct in her conversations with God. "You got me married to this man, this weak and indecisive man, who will make nothing of himself unless I do it. I didn't have a lot of options, did I God? Well, running this household through this man is no harder than watering ten camels. So if you wanted a weaker woman for this man, why ten camels? Two camels would have got you a nice mousy woman for this man."

And Rebecca laughed a little, and went about doing what she knew she had to do, making the best of whatever was.

Esau
who doesn't know how to tell a lie

Introduction

"Nice guys finish last." I don't know who said that, but it is true in the case of Esau.

It all started at day one. Esau is born covered in red hair (his name means "hairy" or "shaggy"), with Jacob, his twin, hanging on to his heel. Esau is a genuinely nice guy, who feels most at home out in the open hunting the game that his father, Isaac, loves to eat. Esau is a man without guile. His emotions are strong and spontaneous, whether he's crying and pleading for some food or for the inheritance that belongs to him, or whether, as later in the story, he's blazing angry and determined to kill Jacob.

But he also forgives. Jacob, and Rebecca their mother, trick blind old Isaac and steal the birthright that should have come to Esau as the eldest twin. Years later, Esau invites Jacob to come back and live with him in the land of Seir.

The story in the Bible – *a paraphrase of Genesis 25:27–34*

When the twins Jacob and Esau grew up, Esau was an excellent hunter, who liked to be out in the open. Jacob was much more quiet, and tended to stay at home. Their father Isaac, who had a taste for wild game, loved Esau. But their mother, Rebecca, loved Jacob.

One day, Jacob was cooking a stew. Just then, Esau came home from the fields feeling absolutely famished. "Jacob," said Esau. "Let me have some of that red stuff you're cooking there. I'm so hungry I could eat anything."

"Well," said Jacob. "I'll let you have some of my stew if you give me the family inheritance."

"Look, I'm dying of hunger," said Esau. "What good is the family inheritance to me?"

"Promise me first," said Jacob. So Esau promised, and in the process sold his birthright to Jacob.

Then Jacob gave Esau some bread and lentil stew. Esau ate and drank and went back out into the fields. Esau didn't care about his birthright.

Why I wrote this story

I sat beside Bruno Engler in the car as we drove through the mountains near Banff. He smelled of the outdoors. And the picture that came into my mind was the scene when old, blind Isaac is ready to give the blessing to his son. Jacob has put on Esau's clothes, so that when he comes to his father to kiss him, Isaac smells the outdoors.

Bruno reminded me of Esau in other ways. He is an internationally recognized guide and photographer, but as we hiked through the bush, I sensed that he was most at home where he could smell the pine and hear the rush of glacial streams.

Bruno, who was born in Switzerland, knew how to swear. His swearing was original and creative and appropriate to the situation – not the mindless repetition of a few obscenities. When we climbed over the Columbia Ice Fields, one of his crampons, the spikes attached to shoes to give traction on the ice, broke. Genuinely angry, Bruno called into question the ancestry, virility, intelligence, and integrity of everyone in Switzerland where the crampons had been made, and did so in all four official languages!

I didn't have the opportunity to get to know Bruno very well, but I had the strong impression that, like Esau, he had no capacity for deceit. At least, that is how I have imagined both of them – men who say what they feel, and do what they do. And who simply don't know how to be dishonest.

It is sad, but people like Esau don't usually do that well. Sooner or later, they encounter a Jacob.

"At least Dad is on my side"

Do you know what it's like when you've been out in the bush all week? And you've caught nothing. Not a thing?

Well, Jacob sure doesn't know about that. Fat, pampered mama's boy, that's what he is. Mom always liked him best. And she put him up to it. Mom is always figuring out ways to get things for Jacob.

I didn't sell my birthright. I was conned. I was cheated.

Do you know what it's like when you come home, and you've

been out hiking around all week? There's hardly any game, and by the time you see any, you're so weak you can't shoot straight. Sure I found a few berries to eat, but all I got out of that was a case of diarrhea.

So I come home. I can hardly walk, I'm so hungry. And Jacob has been sitting around at home with Mom, stirring a pot full of some red stuff. I don't know what it is, but I know I need it and I need it fast.

But Jacob's being coy. "Hey, big brother. How much will you give me for some of my stew?" I try to grab it from him, but he jumps away. "Just give me something to eat, for cryin' out loud, Jacob, I'm starving!"

"So how about the inheritance, Esau. Tell me that, when Pop dies, I get everything. Say that, and I'll give you some of this delicious lentil stew."

"Whatever you want. Give me something to eat!"

That's what happened. I was cheated, right?

And Jacob's been rubbing my nose in that so-called promise ever since. "A promise is a promise," he keeps saying.

"Look, you pampered brat," I grabbed him by the collar and yelled right into his fat little face. "The birthright is for father to give, and father will give it to *me*. So stop being such a smartass!" I would have punched him in the nose but that's when mother came along.

"Esau. You let go of your brother. Just because you're older, it doesn't mean you can lord it over him."

"Well, Mom, you tell him to stop going on with that crap about me selling him my inheritance for a bowl of that red garbage he calls food."

I might as well have been talking to the tent pegs. Mom was totally on Jacob's side. "A promise is a promise, Esau," she says to me. "Remember, your word is your bond."

I know I shouldn't have done it, but that's when I started to yell at her. "Mom, I know Jacob is your pet. OK, but Dad is still on my side, and when the time comes, he will give the inheritance to me, and then you and this pampered pip-squeak will be out on your ear. Just remember that, Mom."

Well, I guess I told 'em. They haven't said anything about it since. And poor Dad is getting old and blind, and pretty soon it'll be time for him to pass on the family blessing to me.

Then I'll show them. I'll really show them.

Leah
the substitute bride

Introduction

The name Leah means "gazelle," but she wasn't. It's Rachel, her younger sister, who was the gazelle, the beautiful one whom everyone loved. Leah was not much to look at. She had weak eyes, and to put it bluntly, nobody was likely to choose her for a bride. Leah knew it.

Leah was one of the daughters of Laban when Jacob, Laban's nephew, arrived on the scene. Jacob immediately fell in love with Rachel. But he had a problem. He had left home in a bit of hurry, running from his brother Esau who wanted to kill him. So he had no money for the bride price. He struck a deal with Laban. Seven years of work for the hand of Rachel.

But Laban pulled a fast one. On the wedding night, Jacob found himself married to Leah, not to Rachel. He got to marry Rachel too, but had to work another seven years.

Leah had many babies, which in that time and culture was considered really wonderful. Rachel didn't. And so there was tension between the sisters.

The story in the Bible – *a paraphrase of Genesis 29:15–31*

Laban said to Jacob. "Just because you are my nephew, it doesn't mean you should work for me for nothing. What kind of wages would you consider fair?"

Laban had two daughters. Leah, the older, had weak eyes, but Rachel had a graceful body. She was beautiful. And Jacob loved Rachel.

"Uncle Laban," he said, "I will work for you for seven years, if you let me marry Rachel."

"I would rather she married you than any other man. It's a deal."

So Jacob worked for Laban for seven years, though it seemed to him as if it was only a few days – he was so much in love with Rachel.

At the end of the seven years, Jacob said. "Give me Rachel, so that I can go to bed with her. I've done my seven years."

Laban agreed, and invited everyone to come for a big wedding feast. But at night, he brought the veiled Leah to Jacob, and that's who he took to bed that night. (Laban gave Leah his maid Zilpah as a present.)

When morning came, Jacob realized it was Leah! "What are you trying to do to me? I worked for you for seven years to earn Rachel. You've ripped me off!"

"Relax," said Laban. "Look, here in our country, the oldest daughter has to be married before the younger sisters. So, have your honeymoon with Leah, then in a week, I'll give you Rachel. And you can work another seven years to earn her."

That's what Jacob did. He completed the week with Leah, and then Laban gave him Rachel as a wife. (Laban then gave his maid Bilhah to Rachel as a wedding gift.)

So Jacob went to bed with Rachel, and he loved her a lot more than Leah. And he worked for Laban for another seven years.

When God saw that Leah wasn't loved, he gave her lots of babies. But Rachel couldn't even get pregnant.

Why I wrote this story

My heart ached for Leah. I tried to imagine what it might be like to be used, manipulated, put down, the way she was. I couldn't. And even having written this story, I doubt I really got to the depth of her feelings.

Or did she simply accept her lot? One way to cope is simply to resign yourself to things. Perhaps Leah was so much a child of her time and culture, she didn't know how to feel, much less express the pain.

I've seen that kind of dull resignation on some faces. I've seen women and men so caught in the web of their unhappy circumstances that they've cut the pain circuits in their minds and learned to push themselves, without feeling, through the necessary functions of daily living. But what a waste of life!

As the story of Leah moves along through the next few chapters of Genesis, we read that God's heart was with Leah. God provided her with babies, which in her time and culture gave Leah enormous satisfaction and status. Sometimes, not always, but sometimes,

Leah: the substitute bride 79

people who are treated shabbily by everyone else, learn how to lean on God.

"I talk to God a lot"

I will never forget Jacob's eyes.

It had been a joyous night for me. Murmurs, gentle touch, contented sleep. His arm resting quietly under my head, his breath soft on my veiled cheek.

Just as the morning light brought its glow into our tent, Jacob woke, and looked at me. I saw tenderness and love in his dark eyes. Then he lifted my veil and the look of love turned to disgust and anger.

"What the blazes?" Jacob yelled. "What are you doing here?"

I knew it would be like this. I told my father, Laban, that it wouldn't work. Jacob would despise me. He wouldn't listen.

"It's your only chance," Laban said. "You're no spring chicken, Leah, and you have those gawd-awful eyes, and if I don't get you married to Jacob you'll be an old maid. An old maid, Leah, who nobody wants and nobody cares about."

"No," I said. "It's not right."

"Leah," said Laban. "I'm your father and I have decided. You will wear a heavy veil, and I'll keep your sister Rachel hidden away, and we'll marry you off to Jacob. After a few glasses of wine, he won't know the difference. You have no say in the matter. Now shut up and do as you are told."

I did as I was told. A woman, especially an ugly woman, has no rights. Still I couldn't help feeling like a piece of slightly tainted meat my father was trying to sell to some unsuspecting buyer.

But somehow, as father worked on the plan to trick Jacob, I began to fantasize that maybe Jacob might love me after all. Maybe the wedding night would be a night of love, and he might, at least, not despise me. It was silly of course. But I don't have much to live on, except my fantasies.

Jacob stormed out of the tent that morning, as I guess I knew he would. And I could hear snippets of angry arguments from father's tent most of the next day. In the end, my father agreed that Jacob could marry Rachel too, but he'd have to work another seven years to pay for her, just as he had already worked seven years to pay for me, the ugly bride he didn't want.

I tried to be a good wife. When Jacob came into my tent to do his duty as a husband, I tried so hard to be kind, to be gentle, to be loving. But I knew he never came to me in love.

I would have died, I think, except for God. I talked to God a lot. I cried a lot at night, and in the tears I found some comfort. I complained about my eyes, grumbled about my lot in life, and prayed that I could have the babies Jacob wanted. And they came, my little blessings. Beautiful boys. I thought that would make Jacob love me, but it didn't work. Maybe that's why I made those snooty remarks to my pretty younger sister. It was the only time in our whole lives when I had something and she didn't.

It took some years, some tears, and much prayer, before finally I told Rachel I was sorry. I'm glad we're friends again. I was with her when she finally had a baby – little Joseph. But she was older now and older women have a hard time having babies. And when Benjamin was born – well Rachel gave her life to have that baby. It broke my heart to lose my sister, and it broke Jacob's heart to lose the woman he had loved so deeply and so long.

One night Jacob came to my bed again. But instead we talked and talked and cried and laughed a little as we shared our grief. And for a little while at least, I knew that in a different kind of way, he loved me too.

And so I am content. I have my children. And Jacob has become, if not a husband who loves me, then at least a friend. And I talk to God a lot.

I am content.

Jacob
the swindler who wrestles with God

Introduction

He's downright embarrassing. Imagine having a liar and a cheat as one of the founders of the great Judaic faith tradition. The Hebrews often referred to themselves as "The House of Jacob" and the new name which Jacob acquired, Israel, became the name of the biblical kingdom and the modern State of Israel. Embarrassing!

And refreshing. One of the many great gifts of Judaism is that the tradition never tried to whitewash its heroes. They were fully, completely, and delightfully human, and Jacob was more human than most.

We know his fascinating story in considerable detail. The sibling rivalry with Esau begins while they are in Rebecca's womb. He cheats Esau out of the family inheritance, lies to his father, swindles his uncle, sees visions of angels on staircases, wrestles with God. His sons sell their brother into slavery. When he dies at the age of 147, Jacob's elaborate funeral cortege carries him all the way from Egypt back home to Hebron.

This is the tiny part of the saga that occurs when Jacob spends the night by the river Jabbok, perhaps struggling with his conscience. He has just swindled his Uncle Laban so he can't go back there. His brother Esau, whom he cheated many years before, is coming to meet him. Jacob is between a rock and a hard place.

He has sent his family and his flocks ahead. Jacob is very alone.

The story in the Bible – *a paraphrase of Genesis 32:24–32*

Jacob was left alone for the whole night. In the darkness, Jacob wrestled with someone or something.

When the unknown wrestler realized he couldn't out-wrestle Jacob, he hit Jacob in the socket of his hip. Jacob's hip was wrenched out of joint.

Then the man said to Jacob. "Let me go. It is almost daylight."

"No," said Jacob. "I won't unless you give me your blessing."

"What is your name?" asked the man.

"Jacob."

"From now on, you won't be called Jacob. You will be called Israel, [which means, "he struggles with God"] because you have struggled with God and with humans, and you have won."

"What is *your* name?"

"Why do you ask?" Then the man blessed Jacob.

Jacob decided to call that place Peniel [the face of God], because "I've seen God face to face, and I'm still alive." The sun rose, as Jacob walked from Peniel, but he limped because of his hip.

That is why, until this day, people of Israel don't eat the tendon on the hip socket, because that's where Jacob was injured.

Why I wrote this story

This is one of those unsettling stories where mythology and history intertwine. Psychiatrist Carl Jung, who spent a lifetime studying dreams and myths and what he called "the collective unconscious," identified this story as one of those which occurs over and over in the myths of many cultures and in the dreams of many individuals.

The dream of wrestling with mysterious, unknown forces, is a dream many of us have had. It is the shadow side of ourselves struggling to come to terms with conflicting values and drives inside ourselves.

I wrote this story of Jacob's struggle because I know his struggle personally. There have been many, many times when conflicting values, conflicting agendas, conflicting ideologies have struggled within me. Most recently, I struggled with yet another "mid-life" crisis, or more accurately a 2/3-life crisis on my 60th birthday. I have the idea that I will live to the age of 90, which means I am now into the "last third." So what am I going to do with it? Between the call of my career which feeds my over-large ego and the calls of quality of life and relationships, I have spent a few sleepless nights wrestling.

But like Jacob, I find myself blessed, even though I walk limping into my future.

"The one who struggles with God"

Jacob knew it would be a restless night. He was given to dreams, to nights of tossing and turning, and waking in the morning not knowing whether it was a dream or a vision or a nightmare or hallucination or simply too much spice on the meat and a bit too much wine to drink.

And Jacob knew that God would speak to him through dreams or visions or whatever it was that happened during those long and restless nights. Especially when things were falling apart in his life. Especially when he was afraid.

And Jacob was afraid. Afraid for his life.

But it was getting dark and tomorrow would be a hard day and somehow he just had to get some rest. There was Esau, his angry brother, to face tomorrow.

Jacob was on his way back home because, well, God had told him in one of those dreams, or visions, or whatever – told him to go home.

Home. Where is home? He had left his mother's house 15 years before, running for his life. Jacob had cheated his brother out of the family inheritance. When Esau threatened to kill him, Jacob ran before he could collect that inheritance, ran off to some distant relatives in a country called Haran. There he managed, through hard work and a fair bit of cheating, to acquire two wives, a bunch of kids, a bundle of servants, and who knows how many sheep and goats and camels. He'd come to Haran with nothing but the shirt on his back. Now he was a wealthy man, but he couldn't go back to Haran either because he had also swindled his Uncle Laban.

"Where can I go, God?" Jacob demanded. "My brother Esau and my Uncle Laban are both angry enough to kill me."

"Go home," said God.

Jacob's stomach churned. His head ached. "I've got to get some rest," he muttered to himself, as he laid a blanket over the sharp rocks and prickly bushes of the unrelenting desert.

The last rays of sun faded from the cloudless sky as Jacob dozed a little. Fitfully. Finally, he fell into a troubled sleep.

Then into his sleep or vision came a stranger, a man, a someone. And Jacob wrestled with the man, wrestled and struggled, hour after hour, straining for every small advantage, every muscle, every sinew stressed. And then the stranger reached and pressed, and

Jacob screamed as waves of pain shot from his hip throughout his body.

But Jacob held on. Held on with every fiber, held on, knowing somehow beyond the knowing that this was a struggle for life itself, knowing that this wrestling was a battle for his very soul.

"Let me go!" said the stranger. "It will soon be dawn. I have to go."

"Bless me!" Jacob screamed. "Bless me!"

Something changed just then. Jacob sensed that now the stranger's death grip changed to an embrace.

"What is your name?" The voice was gentle.

"My name is Jacob."

"What does your name mean?"

"It means...it means I am a cheater. I take what isn't mine."

"Now, Jacob. Now you have a new name. Your name is Israel— Israel, the one who struggles with God—the one who knows God in the stress of life. And not your name only, but the name of all your children, all God's children through the ages shall be known as Israel, the people who struggle with God."

Jacob stood to meet the dawn and screamed in pain. His hip was out of joint, and Jacob knew that whether it was dream or vision, he had indeed struggled with God, struggled with himself, and from the struggle, God was calling him toward a way of being he could hardly understand much less explain.

Jacob faced the rising sun, and faced the pain that throbbed his new name "Israel" hard into his mind. Israel, the wounded people who struggle with their God.

Then Jacob, Israel, walked limping to the future.

Potiphar's wife
a dysfunctional boy and a bored woman

Introduction

Joseph is certainly one of the romantic characters in the Bible, and plenty of stories have been written about him. He lived in about the 16th century, BCE, the 11th son (the daughters are simply not mentioned) of Jacob and the first child of Rachel. The other children were by Jacob's other wife, Leah, and by several concubines.

Joseph's mother, Rachel, died during the birth of Benjamin, her second child. And Joseph's father pampered him, giving him a colorful, long-sleeved cloak, a symbol showing that he did not need to work. The family did not get along, and Joseph found himself sold into slavery in Egypt where he lived by his wits and by his faith in God.

Potiphar bought Joseph from the slave traders, and that set the scene for this story. Potiphar was a captain of the Pharaoh's guard, which was about the equivalent of being the Minister of Defense in today's government. We know almost nothing about him, and even less about his wife.

The story in the Bible – *a paraphrase of Genesis 37:36, 39:1–23*

And the Midianites took Joseph to Egypt, where they sold him as a slave to Potiphar, who was captain of Pharaoh's guard.

Now God stood by Joseph and helped him. It was evident that whatever he did worked out. Potiphar noticed, and found himself liking Joseph. So Potiphar made him the head of his household, And sure enough, everything that Joseph did seemed to work out.

Things went well in Potiphar's house while Joseph was in charge. God looked after Joseph the whole time. Joseph looked after everything, except the food that Potiphar ate.

Joseph was well-built and very handsome. And after awhile, Potiphar's wife began to notice Joseph, and she said, "Come to bed with me." But he said, "No. Listen, I work for Potiphar. He's made me responsible for everything. I'm in charge of this whole household. He's given me access to everything. Except you, of course. So how could I do such a terrible thing? It would be a sin against God."

She kept at him, every day, but he paid no attention to her. She kept trying to get him into bed with her.

One day, Joseph went into the house to do his work. Nobody else was in the house at the time, except Potiphar's wife. She grabbed his clothes and said, "Go to bed with me!" But he pulled away and ran off, and left her holding his cloak.

Then she yelled for the other people around, and she said, "Look at this. Potiphar brought this Hebrew here to make fun of us. He came in here and tried to rape me. That's why I started yelling. So he got scared and ran, and I grabbed his cloak. See!"

Later, when Potiphar came home, she told him, "That Hebrew servant you brought in here – he figured he could have a good time with me. So I yelled for help, and he ran off leaving his cloak behind."

That got Potiphar very angry. He threw Joseph into jail and might have had him killed if God hadn't been looking out for him.

In fact, God helped Joseph make a good impression on the jailer, and before long Joseph was in charge of the whole prison. The jailer trusted Joseph completely.

Why I told this story

It's the victors who get to write the history. It was the descendants of Joseph who wrote the story of what happened in his encounter with Potiphar's wife.

I got to wondering about that when I saw the Andrew Lloyd Webber and Tim Rice production of *Joseph and the Technicolor Dream Coat*. Potiphar's wife is the villain there too. She is simply a wealthy sex kitten.

Like so many biblical women, she doesn't have a name. And we've never heard her version of what happened. I have a strong hunch there's more to the story than we read in the Bible.

Think of it this way. Joseph comes from a desperately dysfunctional family. Having been sold as a slave, he might have, as they say "a few unresolved issues." She is a member of the Egyptian nobility, and probably pampered and bored. What happens if you put two such people together?

One day in a storytelling workshop, I asked that question. A 30-something woman stood up and retold the story, as if *she* were Potiphar's wife. Her intensity was electrifying. "I know. I *am* Potiphar's wife."

I can still hear her voice in my head. My retelling is in the spirit of the story I heard that day.

"Joseph had to pay the price. But so did I!"

It all depends on who you believe, I guess. I didn't tell my side very well, and even my husband Potiphar didn't really believe me. Oh, I know. He said he did. He had to for the sake of his pride and politics. I come from a powerful family too, and it wouldn't do for Potiphar to publicly accuse me of adultery.

He didn't accuse me privately either, except with his eyes. Except with his body. In fact, Potiphar was more upset about losing Joseph than he was about anything I might have done. No, of course he didn't say that. But a woman knows these things.

Whatever you may have heard about this ugly affair, you need to know it wasn't as simple as the stories that got passed around Egypt. It was not just Joseph trying to get me into bed, or me getting the hots for a young hunk.

Joseph was very good looking and a charmer, and he knew it. In fact, sometimes he was an arrogant twit. He was also a lonely, frightened mixed-up kid. His family was so messed up. His brothers had grabbed him one day when they were out with the flocks and they beat up on him and threw him into a deep hole. Then, when some Midianite traders came along, they sold him as a slave.

That's how he came into my house. Potiphar bought him at the slave market. I remember noticing him when Potiphar's guard brought him into the courtyard. They gave him a good whipping, something they always did with a new slave. "That's for *nothing*," said Potiphar. "Just think of what you'll get if you do *something*."

Joseph cried and yelled under the whipping. And I wanted to run out to him – to hold him and comfort him like the child that he was. He seemed too small and vulnerable.

But he was also very clever. And it took him almost no time to learn a few words of Egyptian. He worked hard. Very hard. I think he worked so hard because he was so afraid, and working was the only thing that made the fear stop. Potiphar couldn't see all that of course. Potiphar just saw a good, hard-working slave, and so gradually Joseph got more responsibility, more independence, and even power.

Power over Potiphar. Joseph spoke fluent Egyptian in a couple of years. He spoke so beautifully to Potiphar. "Wooed" him. Yes, that's the word. He never flattered Potiphar. But Joseph sprinkled his speech with flattering inferences, especially when talking to the other servants. And of course it got back to Potiphar. As the teenage kid became a young man, he had Potiphar wound around his little finger. Joseph wooed him as a lover might – stroked him with his compliments and softened him with thoughtfulness.

Potiphar put him in charge of everything. "You are in charge of my whole household," Potiphar said grandly. "Except for my food, which you must not touch because you are not Egyptian and therefore unclean." I wondered at the time if "whole household" included me.

Joseph enjoyed his power. He ordered Potiphar's tailor to make him a coat. "A coat of many colors – and with long sleeves," he ordered. "But not quite as nice as Potiphar's," he added. "That would be an insult to my kind and gentle master. Almost as nice, but not quite."

Joseph loved to boss the other slaves around, and often treated them more harshly than Potiphar. He called them "dirty slaves" sometimes, forgetting I think, that he was still a slave himself.

I forgot he was a slave. Because he was in charge, Joseph no longer had to work with his hands so he could wear his long-sleeved colored cloak. There was no getting away from it. He cut a handsome figure and he knew it.

I had time on my hands. My God, I had time on my hands. There were banquets and royal functions to go to, and some entertaining, but other than keeping myself beautiful for those occasions, I had nothing to do. So Joseph and I talked.

Oh my, we talked. About everything. And as we talked, we became closer. More vulnerable to each other. Sometimes he was a little boy again, a terribly mixed-up and frightened little boy, a little boy who missed his mother terribly, a little boy who needed to be cuddled, a little boy who had learned to survive by his wits but whose fearful motto was, "Do unto others before they do you."

Joseph had an almost desperate need to be loved, though he would not admit it. But there was a cold, calculating, fearful side as well, and it frightened me. The way he talked with steel-eyed detachment about his family – his brothers – just sent shivers up my spine.

I don't know who he thought I was. A spoiled brat? A rich bitch? For one thing, I was old enough to be that mother who had died in childbirth with his brother Benjamin. Sometimes Joseph talked to me as he might have talked to his mother. Joseph needed a mother.

I didn't need an adult son. I'm not sure what I needed, but I didn't want to be his mother.

I grew up wealthy and pampered – a snotty kid from a rich family where you get everything you want and nothing that you really need. Potiphar didn't love me. Our wedding was arranged by our fathers. The first time I saw him was on our wedding day. He was impotent. Frightened, I guess. So was I, for that matter. Things got a little better as we got to know each other, but not much. Potiphar and I had what you might call, an arrangement of convenience. We did all the right things publicly, but privately we mostly ignored each other.

Both of us were desperately lonely. Potiphar would never have admitted that, and I didn't know it until Joseph and I began to have real conversations. You don't know what you've missed until you have it. Or until you lose it.

I didn't plan to get involved sexually with Joseph. The thought had crossed my mind and my body, but I had suppressed it. The consequences of adultery in Egypt were too frightening to even think about. And I'm not sure how it happened, but the afternoon was hot and we were inside where it was cooler. Joseph and I had talked for several hours. Then we ate and drank some wine.

I was embroidering. It helps when you are bored to keep your hands moving at least. I poked my finger with a needle, and I winced. Joseph, with all that charm he could turn on so easily, said, "Let me kiss it better," and the next thing I knew we were kissing each other and fondling each other and taking our clothes off.

Then I heard the door slam and I knew one of the other slaves was coming into the house. Joseph heard it too and ran, and there

I was, half dressed, with Joseph's many-colored cloak on the floor beside me as the slave walked in. I panicked.

"Help!" I screamed. "Joseph tried to rape me. Joseph tried to rape me. Get Potiphar, quick. Tell him Joseph tried to rape me."

I ran into my room and slammed the door and cried and screamed and pounded on my pillow. Then I knew what I had done to Joseph. Potiphar would have to kill him. Or send him to jail at least. And there was nothing I could do about it.

Even if I went to Potiphar and told the truth. Potiphar would have his honor to protect. Joseph had to pay the price.

But so did I. So did I.

Joseph
a spoiled kid brother

Introduction

The incident with Potiphar's wife is Joseph's only big slip-up in his legendary career. He was tossed in jail, but there he interpreted the dreams of fellow prisoners and that eventually got him interpreting the dreams of the Pharaoh himself.

It was commonly believed that dreams could foretell the future. And Pharaoh's dream, as interpreted by Joseph, predicted seven years of good crops and seven years of famine. That interpretation earned Joseph the position of Prime Minister. He was in charge of everything, and immediatly built storage facilities to stockpile food from the bumper crops for the seven years of drought.

The famine hit not only Egypt but the whole region. People came from all over to buy food in Egypt, and that included Joseph's brothers.

That's where they encountered their brother whom they had sold as a slave. Of course, they didn't recognize him.

The story in the Bible – *a paraphrase of Genesis 45:1–15*

Joseph just couldn't control himself any longer in front of all the Egyptian courtiers. So he yelled, "Get everyone out of here!" There was no one else around when Joseph made himself known to his brothers, but he cried so loudly, that everyone in the whole Egyptian court heard it. Even Pharaoh's household heard it.

Joseph said to his brothers. "It's me. I am Joseph. Is Dad still alive?" His brothers of course were totally overwhelmed and terrified. They couldn't say a word.

Then Joseph said, "Come here. Come closer." The brothers moved closer to where Joseph was sitting. "I am your brother. Joseph. The same brother you sold as a slave into Egypt. Don't get upset. Don't be too hard on yourselves because you did this. Because God sent me ahead of you here, to help keep us all alive. We've had a famine, as you know, for two years, and there are five more years to go before the crops come back. God sent me ahead, to keep you and our family alive. So, you see, it wasn't you who put me here. It was God. God has made me a kind of father to Pharaoh. I'm in charge of his whole house, and I'm ruler over the whole land of Egypt.

"So, hurry home and tell my father. Tell him God has made me the most powerful person in Egypt. Tell him to come here, right away. You all can settle in the land of Goshen, so you'll be nice and close by. You, and your children, and your grandchildren, and all your herds and flocks. Everybody and everything. I'll make sure you have enough to eat because there are still five more years before the famine is over. I don't want you and the whole family to be hungry and poor.

"So you see it with your own eyes, eh. You see it too, Benjamin. It really is me that is talking to you. Please tell Dad that I am a big name in Egypt. Tell him everything you've seen here. So hurry up. Bring father and the whole clan out here."

Then Joseph threw his arms around his brother Benjamin and cried. He hugged and kissed his other brothers, and there were lots of tears.

And after that, Joseph and his brothers had a long talk.

Why I wrote this story

It was the last half of verse 15. "...and after that his brothers talked with him."

What did they talk about? Because the relationship of Joseph and his brothers was, to put it mildly, dysfunctional. They hated each other. Joseph had been the smart-ass kid who taunted his older brothers – half-brothers actually, except for Benjamin – taunted them with his fancy clothes and his ability to interpret dreams. They retaliated by plotting to kill him, then sold him as a slave. They figured he was dead, and good riddance. Suddenly Joseph popped up holding the power of life and death over them. You don't need to be a psychiatrist to see there are a few unresolved issues here.

I hope they really talked. Not the pious little speeches of the kind Joseph made in the text as we have it. Such family issues take hours and days and weeks and months to work through, and sometimes never are. It's a faint hope, because men don't usually do this very well. But I fantasized that maybe these 12 men might have matured enough, cared enough, to walk that painful road together.

"I am your brother. Do you remember me?"

The sobs heaved out of his body. One after another, his large, muscular frame was wracked with grief and pain he'd never known himself to feel. Until this moment.

Joseph had never known how to cry. His life had been a struggle to survive, to prevail, to prosper, to overcome. Joseph survived on his wits. He was the only Hebrew in the Egyptian court, and his very life depended on his ability to be one jump ahead of everyone else. There was no time, no room for weakness, ever. Certainly no time for tears.

But now he was weak. Curled up like a small boy on the edge of his ornate official chair, Joseph wept the tears he should have wept all through his troubled life.

Joseph wept the tears of anger. Anger at his abusive brothers, who years before had beat him, stripped him of his long-sleeved cloak, thrown him in a pit, and sold him into slavery. Anger at the Egyptians for whom he had slaved, whom he had outwitted, and over whom he now ruled. Anger at himself, for the spoiled-brat younger brother he had been, for all the lies he told and all the people he had used.

Joseph wept the tears of loneliness and fear. Torn from his family, thrown into slavery, no love, no affection, no affirmation, nothing but his own wits and studied determination to carry him into each terrifying day.

Now his brothers stood before him. His *brothers*. These were his own flesh and blood – the ones who had abused and sold him. He should hate and punish them. But in spite of himself, Joseph wanted nothing in the world more than to be loved by his brothers. And his father. Oh, how he yearned for the affection of his father.

His brothers stood before him. Confused. Afraid. They had no idea this Egyptian official was the brother they had betrayed.

"Get out of here," Joseph shouted through his tears to all the Egyptians in the room. "Get out. I want to be alone with these men."

Then he turned on his brothers. "I am Joseph. I am your little brother. Do you perhaps remember me?" They dropped to the ground, terrified.

Then the hiss of his first challenge broke. "Is father still alive?" Only Judah managed to raise his head enough to nod a wary "yes" to Joseph's plea.

Again the tears. Joseph knew how much he wanted to be loved, to be accepted by his brothers. And yet his anger at them boiled inside.

"It's all right, my brothers." In his desperate need for love, Joseph stifled his anger and told the pious lie. "God arranged it all. God knew there'd be a famine in the land, so God put me here in the Egyptian court so I could take care of you and my father and our whole tribe. It wasn't your fault, you see!"

Joseph walked up to Benjamin, his youngest brother, and embraced him. "Ben, Ben. It is so good to see you. How is Dad? Tell me how my father is?"

Benjamin swallowed hard. "He's fine. Just fine."

"Tell Dad that I'm alive. I'm okay. And tell him that I've done real well. Tell him I'm in charge of just about everything here, that I'm second-in-command to Pharaoh. Tell him that, will you Ben?"

Ben nodded, still dazed. Joseph wondered why he'd said that. Why was it so important to have his Dad know of his success?

It took days before Joseph and his brothers cut through years of fear and anger and repression to really talk with each other. One day, Joseph found again the anger he had hidden, enough that he could shout his rage. "Why did you do that to me?" For which there was, of course, no longer any answer.

Then one day there was confession. One by one the brothers, Joseph too, found words to name their sins. One by one they asked forgiveness from each other and from God. One by one they vowed to purge their lives of jealousy and greed that brought them to such deeds.

Now the tears flowed freely. And sometimes laughter too, as brothers saw each other now as fragile, lonely men who needed more than anything the care and love that only they could give each other.

"The God of our ancestors did not lead us to abuse and to betray you, Joseph," Judah said one day. "Our God is a just and loving God, and would never will such things. But God has used our weakness and our sin and through it has brought life to Egypt and to our father's clan. Thanks be to God."

"Thanks be to God," repeated Joseph and his brothers.

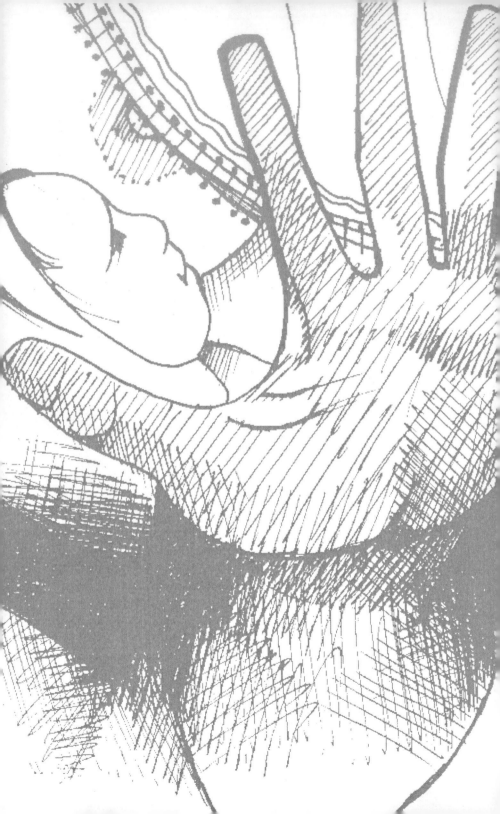

Pharaoh's daughter
the fear was gone

Introduction

We know almost nothing about Pharaoh's daughter. Like most biblical women, she is known by who she "belongs" to, not by a name. The other women in this story are named in other places. For instance, Miriam, the sister, played a prominent role in the saga of the liberation of the Hebrews.

Insofar as this story has a historical base, the Pharaoh's daughter was the child of Rameses II, who ruled Egypt between 1,301 and 1,234 BCE. But many of the elements of this story are similar to other birth legends of the time. Sargon of Agade, who lived about 2,600 BCE, has a similar birth narrative.

Such legends are very useful to us, because they are told in such sparse language that we feel free to imagine all the details in the theater of our own minds, and in that way connect them to our own experience.

In this story, the baby Moses is hidden because the Pharaoh has issued a decree that all male Hebrew babies are to be killed. Pharaoh is concerned about the overpopulation of the Hebrews, and is afraid that in the event of a war, they might fight with the enemy.

The story in the Bible – *a paraphrase of Exodus 2:1–10*

A man from the priestly house of Levi got married to a woman of the same tribe. She became pregnant and had a son. When they saw that he was a fine boy, they hid him from the soldiers for three months. When the family couldn't hide the baby any longer, the mother got a reed basket, and she smeared it with pitch to seal it.

Then she put the baby boy into the basket and put it in the reeds by the side of the river. The boy's older sister stood at a distance to look out for the boy.

Pharaoh's daughter came down to take a bath in the river, while her attendants stood on the bank and watched. She noticed the basket among the reeds and ordered one of her servants to go and get it for her. The child was crying, and she felt sorry for him. "This must be one of the Hebrew babies," she said.

Then the baby's sister ran up and said, "Would you like me to get you a woman to nurse this child for you?"

"Yes," said Pharaoh's daughter. So the girl went and called the baby's mother.

"Take this child and feed it for me. I'll pay you for it."

So the woman took the baby and nursed it. When the child grew up, she took him to the palace to Pharaoh's daughter, who then adopted him as her son. She named him "Moses," because, she said, "I drew him out of the water."

Why I wrote this story

You can blame it all on George Gershwin who (in 1935) took a story by Dorothy and DuBose Heyward about African-American life on the Charleston waterfront, and made it into the folk opera, *Porgy and Bess*. That opera contains a wonderful song, *It Ain't Necessarily So* which quite explicitly calls into question many of the biblical stories. That includes this story of the birth of Moses and Pharaoh's daughter. "She found him, *she says*" in a basket in the river.

Porgy and Bess was written near the time I was born. During that era, sexual ethics were changing, but pity the poor girl who got "caught." Shotgun weddings, sudden long trips to visit an obscure aunt, and worst of all, back-alley abortions were the usual "solution." Girls were expected to come to their wedding beds as virgins. Men were expected to "sow a few wild oats" before they settled down.

Under this oppressive double standard, great courage and imagination was often required of women – the ones who found themselves pregnant, and those mothers and sisters who helped them through the trauma. It was this kind of courage that was shown by the women in this story of Moses – the midwives who fooled the Pharaoh, the mother who birthed him and then hid her baby, the sister who watched over him, and the Pharaoh's daughter who adopted him.

Moses, the great leader, like many other great leaders, would simply not have survived without the courageous women who risked their lives so that he might live. As a male, I find it hard to understand that kind of love, nor do I know how much it costs.

"I wish that I could hear my father sing again"

I don't think my father wanted to be a Pharaoh. Not if he'd had a choice. He might have been a musician.

Sometimes, when he would give a banquet, father would bring the best musicians in all Egypt to entertain. And I could tell that father loved the music while he disliked the stuffed-shirts he invited to the banquet. I remember father singing in the hallways sometimes, years ago when I was just a child, before he was a Pharaoh. Once, he even sang to me, a strong and tender song.

I haven't heard him sing for years. They say the head that wears a crown can never sleep too well, and those who cannot sleep will never sing. Father feels such pressure. I know he does. I can see the tiny muscles just below his ears that move when he's afraid.

Those stuffed shirts who run my father's government are feeling pressure from the hordes of Hebrews. I overheard my father and some other men discuss the problem once. "Kick the whole bunch out," one man said. "No," said another. "Who would make our bricks? Who would tend our fields? We need the Hebrews. We just don't need so many. What we need is population control."

Because my father is the Pharaoh, he hardly ever takes his meals with us. He's much too busy. Except every month or two we have a "family time" and we eat a hurried meal together. Father talks to us. We don't talk to father and he hardly looks at us.

"Do you know how strong those Hebrew women are?" he asked us once, not wanting or expecting any answer. "Why, I ordered all the midwives to destroy the male babies just as soon as they are born, but they tell me those Hebrew women just take an hour away from their work, pop out the babies, and go back to work. They just pop them out, and the midwives aren't even needed." Father laughed dryly at his own humor. "They just pop them out."

I glanced up at my mother then, and she was laughing too, but I could tell it wasn't at my father's humor. "He knows nothing," she said later. "He's never seen a baby born."

"But why would father want those babies killed? Is my own father really such a beast?"

"He is a Pharaoh first and always, and a father only sometimes."

Two weeks later, I was bathing in the Nile, enjoying the cool, fresh water on my body, when Lita, one of my servants pointed to a basket in the reeds nearby.

"Bring it to me!"

"It's a baby!" said Lita as she pushed the basket to me. "It's a beautiful Hebrew baby. My mother is a midwife. She told me soldiers throw the Hebrew baby boys into the river now."

"So *this* is a child my brave father fears." I picked the baby up into my arms and held him close. "My father will not hurt you," I said.

The baby cried a little. Then it smiled and tried to suck my finger.

"You will start a rumor," I said to Lita. It was a sudden inspiration, and if I'd stopped to think I might not have said it. "You will whisper in the corridors of the palace that I have been seduced by Scrakum, yes Scrakum, the Prime Minister's son. He's such a stuffed shirt. And this is our child."

Lita grinned. "This is against the Pharaoh's law! But I will help you save the child."

"My father's law, to have these babies killed, is wrong, Lita. Women cannot fight the law, but we can resist."

It took a month to get an audience with my own father.

"Five minutes. No more," said his secretary, smirking at the child in my arms.

"Yes?" said father in his official Pharaoh voice.

"This baby," I said quietly. "You have heard perhaps that it belongs to Scrakum."

"I have heard. I am making arrangements for you to be part of Scrakum's harem. He doesn't want you for a wife. In fact, he claims the child is not his but he is willing to acknowledge it for my sake. All the palace women say the baby looks like Scrakum."

I looked my father in the eye. "The child is Hebrew," I said firmly.

I could see the fear that ran across my father's face. He sensed immediately the derisive laughter in the corridors if it were known that his own daughter had a baby by a Hebrew slave. The tiny muscles near his ears twitched. He took a long, deep drink of wine.

I had been afraid when I came in the room. Now my fear was gone. "I will tell no one, father. I will go join Scrakum's harem, even though he is a pompous ass. But this is one Hebrew child that I will guard with my whole life, and you will not touch him with your wickedness."

"Get out of here!" He meant it to sound hard and firm, but then his Pharaoh's voice croaked in fear.

I pitied him. I pitied him and loved him. And how I wish that I could hear my father sing again.

Zipporah
the fire and the fear

Introduction

The Moses legend is full of puzzles and inconsistencies. The name of Zipporah's father, for instance. Moses married Zipporah in the desert when he was on the run for murdering an Egyptian. Her father is called Reuel in one place, and Jethro in another, and Hobab in a third. I don't even try to reconcile the inconsistencies in this story or any other biblical legend. I simply enjoy the story and accept the wisdom that it offers.

That wisdom may be there in the person of Zipporah. She lived about the 13th century BCE, the daughter of a priest. Zipporah went with Moses back to Egypt when he was called to be God's agent to release the Hebrews, but it appears she returned to Midian at some point to wait for Moses there.

One of the odd, fascinating tidbits in the Bible occurs when she and Moses and their two children are en route to Egypt (Exodus 4:24-26). The text says that God met them and tried to kill Moses. We're not told why. To save his life, Zipporah cut off her son's foreskin and touched Moses "feet" with it, and uttered a strange incantation about a "bridegroom of blood." "Feet" was sometimes a euphemism for genitals.

The incident tells us that Zipporah knew some cultic practices that Moses didn't know, and that the rite of circumcision may have originated with the Midianites.

The story in the Bible – *an abbreviated paraphrase of Exodus 2:15–4:20*

Moses ran away from Pharaoh. He went to the land of Midian, where he sat down by a well.

Now the priest of Midian had seven daughters who came to the well to water their father's animals. There were some shepherds around who chased the women away. Moses stood up and helped the women, and then watered their animals for them.

When the women got back home, their father Reuel asked, "How come you're home so early?"

"An Egyptian helped us fight off the shepherds," said the women. "Then he helped us water the animals."

"Why didn't you bring him home for dinner?"

Moses agreed to come for a meal, and to stay with the family. Reuel gave one of his daughters, Zipporah, to Moses in marriage. She had a baby, and Moses named him Gershom, which means, "I'm a stranger in a foreign land."

Many years later, the king of Egypt died, but the Israelites groaned under their slavery. They cried out, and God heard them. God remembered the promise to Abraham, Isaac, and Jacob.

One day when Moses was out keeping the flocks, an angel of the Lord appeared to him in the form of a bush that burned, but was not consumed. Out of the bush Moses heard a voice. "I am the God of your ancestors, the God of Abraham, Isaac, and Jacob. I have seen the misery of my people in Egypt. I will send you to Pharaoh to bring my people out of slavery."

"But if I go to the Israelites and say, 'The God of our ancestors has sent me,' they will ask, 'What is his name?' What shall I say to them?"

"I AM WHO I AM."

So Moses took his wife and his sons, put them on a donkey, and went back to the land of Egypt. And Moses carried the staff of God in his hand.

Why I wrote this story

If you read the Bible very carefully, you can see a progression of ideas. At first, the patriarchs and matriarchs believed there were many gods, each god looking after one particular tribe or people. Some gods were more powerful than others. Then they began to believe their own God was more powerful than the others. Eventually, the Hebrews came to believe there was really only one God, the god of the Hebrews – and finally, only one God for all of humankind.

The progression was not smooth and neat. But a major milestone on the journey was Moses' encounter with the burning bush. It was a radical idea for Moses – the idea that there really is only one God. Where would he get such an idea?

Some scholars have wondered if perhaps he found it there in Midian. It can be argued that the priest Jethro (or Reuel) had already arrived at that point. But Zipporah, as we have seen, knew something about religion too. Did the idea perhaps come from her?

We'll never know. So we imagine.

"Perhaps there is one god of all the Gods"

There was fire in his eyes when I first saw him. Fire and fear.

My sisters and I had gone to water our sheep at the well, but a gang of men came with their own sheep and wouldn't let us anywhere near the well. That's when this Hebrew came out of nowhere. He yelled at them, fought with their leader, and drove them away.

"Come," he said to my sisters and me, "water your flock."

Father wanted to know how come we got home so much earlier than usual. When we told him, he sent us right back to the well.

"Our father would be honored if you would break bread with us," we said. That's when I saw the fire in his eyes. And the fear.

"And what is your father's name?"

"Our father is Reuel, the priest of Midian. May we tell him your name?"

"I am Moses. I am a Hebrew."

I wondered about that. The Hebrews were slaves and Moses wasn't wearing the clothes of a slave; he was wearing the garments of nobility. But of course I said nothing.

Moses came and ate with us. Father invited him to stay and live, and soon Moses was part of our family. One day Father announced that he had given me to Moses as a wife.

Moses was a good husband. I learned to know and love the fire and the fear that shone through his dark eyes. I saw the fire when he spoke of his people, how they groaned under the slavery of the Egyptian Pharaohs.

"Someday," he said to our first child when he was born, "Someday we shall be free."

I saw the fear when Moses fell sick with fever – sick and near to death. "Why does God attack me?" he demanded. "Why, Zipporah?"

"Moses," I said to him. "I have learned the ways of our desert god. I know the sacrifice of blood. The circumcision of our son shall save you from the wrath of God." This I did, and Moses lived.

He lived, but he was not at peace. The Hebrew slaves in Egypt were always on his mind. Sometimes Moses raged at Pharaoh, raged at all the gods who let the Hebrews suffer under Pharaoh's cruel whip. "Why do the gods permit this?" he would ask.

"Perhaps there is one God of all the gods, Moses," I said to him one day. "My father says that may be so. Could it be that if you called on such a God, this God of gods might come to free your people from their pain?"

Again, the fire and the fear in Moses' eyes. He said nothing to me then, but my thoughts had found their way into his heart – this I could tell. The thought that one great God of gods might lead his people into freedom brought fire into Moses' eyes, and fear into his heart.

One day Moses came home out of the desert, his face was dark and burned as from too much noonday sun. But through that darkened face the fire and the fear burned in his eyes as I had never seen it burn before, and have never seen it since.

"There is a God of all the gods, Zipporah, just as you said there might be." Moses' whisper fairly crackled through our tent. "And I have met this God. I met this God there in the desert, in a bush that burned but was not consumed."

Moses was silent for a long, long time. I knew that he would speak to me when he was ready. Finally, "I am going down to Egypt, Zipporah. I am going to Egypt to tell Pharaoh, 'let my people go.'"

"No, Moses. We'll all be killed."

"You will stay here with your father, Zipporah. I must go to Egypt alone."

"But, but, Moses, why you? Why does it have to be you?" I cried.

"That's what I asked this God. 'Who am I? Why me?' But this God just said, 'I will be with you.'"

"What kind of an answer is that, Moses? You don't even know this God's name."

"I AM!" Moses said that with a fierceness that startled me. I had no idea what he was talking about.

"I AM WHO I AM. I WILL BE WHO I WAS AND WHAT I WILL BECOME. That is God's name."

Again, there was a long silence. I saw the fire and the fear in Moses' eyes. I felt the fire and the fear in my own heart.

"I must go to Egypt, but I am so afraid, Zipporah. I must go, but I don't want to go. Why me? Why did this I AM God call on me?"

Again the silence. I could see through Moses' eyes that this time the fire was the fire of the burning bush that he had seen, and it would overcome his fear.

This time I spoke. "Go Moses. Go to Egypt to confront the Pharaoh. Your child and I will go there with you. Go, Moses. The God who is called I AM will go with you – will give you strength and courage and wisdom – and this God I AM will bring you and your people back to Midian. Go Moses!"

Jonathan
the measure of a man

Introduction

Jonathan is one of the thoroughly likable people in the Bible. He is exuberant and loyal in a way that few biblical men are.

Jonathan was the son of King Saul, the first king of Israel. The story opens with Jonathan leading his platoon into an ill-advised attack on a Philistine garrison. That brought the mass of Philistine troops into Israel – 30,000 of them against the 600 Israelites. What's more, the Philistines had better technology – iron swords against the bronze and stone weapons of the Israelites. But with some daring-do, Jonathan completely spooked the Philistines who turned and ran.

Jonathan was the hero, and Saul was jealous.

Then the story moves to another battle with the Philistines, the famous one where David kills the giant Goliath. David is the hero of the hour and comes to live with Saul and Jonathan. The two young men form an immediate and powerful bond of friendship. Nowhere else in the Bible is the friendship of two men spoken of with such intensity.

The story in the Bible – *selected portions from*
1 Samuel 17:58 to 2 Samuel 1:27

When David returned from the slaughter of Goliath, he was brought before Saul, who wanted to know who he was. "I am the son of Jesse, your servant in Bethlehem," said David.

When Saul had finished talking to David, Jonathan [Saul's son] and David became good friends. Saul would not let David go back to his own home, but insisted that he stay in the king's tent. David and Jonathan became very close friends. Jonathan loved David as much as he loved himself.

Then Jonathan made a covenant, a pledge of eternal friendship with David. He gave David his own robe and his sword and his bow and even his cummerbund as a symbol of this covenant. (1 Samuel 17:58–18:4)

***

David became a famous warrior. A popular hero. There were rumors that he was destined to be the king. Saul became increasingly concerned...

One day, Saul spoke to Jonathan his son, and to all his servants, and wondered if David should be killed. But Jonathan really liked David, so he went and told David about what his father had said. "Go hide till tomorrow," Jonathan said. "Let me talk to my father about you."

So the next day, Jonathan spoke to Saul and said many good things about David. "It would be a sin if you hurt David, because he has done nothing to harm you. Remember, God was with him when he killed Goliath for us. Remember how happy you were when he did that? Would you kill an innocent man?"

Saul heard what Jonathan had said and reconciled himself with David. And David continued to live with Saul as he had before.(1 Samuel 19:1–7)

***

Saul suffered some form of depression. As the depression deepened, Saul's jealousy became an obsession...

Then David found himself on the run again. He said to Jonathan, "What have I done? How have I hurt your father that he wants to kill me."

"Don't worry," said Jonathan. "My father doesn't do anything without telling me. My father won't try to hurt you without talking to me about it first."

"Your father knows how much you like me," said David. "He won't tell you about his plans to kill me. There's only a step between me and death."

"If my father plans anything against you, I will warn you," said Jonathan.

So David and Jonathan made plans to find out what was happening with Saul and to get word to David, so that he could flee if necessary. They promised each other that regardless of what happened, their love for each other would not end.

King Saul was at the banquet held each month at the beginning of the new moon. When it was obvious that David was not in his usual place, he asked Jonathan about it.

"He asked permission to go to Bethlehem because there's a big family event going on."

Saul got very angry when Jonathan said that. "You son-of-a-bitch! I know what's going on between you and that son of Jesse. You're a disgrace to your family. Don't you know that as long as David is around, you will never inherit my throne? Go get him for me and let me kill him."

"What do you want to kill him for? What has he done?"

At that, Saul threw a javelin at Jonathan, who now knew how serious his father was. Jonathan was upset and angry. He grieved for the friendship that he now knew he would lose.

So Jonathan met David at their prearranged rendezvous. They kissed each other and cried together. Finally, Jonathan said to David, "Go in peace. You and I have sworn our loyalty to each other. God will watch between you and me, and between our children, and our children's children.

Then David went out into the wilderness. And Jonathan went back into the city. (1 Samuel 20)

* * *

David lived in the wilderness, hiding out in a mountainous area called Ziph. Saul kept looking for him to kill him, but God wouldn't let him find David.

Jonathan found him though. He said to David, "Don't be afraid. My father won't find you. You will be king of Israel some day, and I will be your second-in-command. My father knows that."

Then David and Jonathan renewed their covenant. David went back to his hideout, and Jonathan went back to his house. (1 Samuel 23:15–18)

* * *

David became a roving warlord, surviving as best he could with a band of about 600 men. Meanwhile the battles with the Philistines continued...

The Philistines fought against Israel and beat them. The men of Israel ran with the Philistines at their heals. Saul's sons, including Jonathan were killed. And so was Saul. (1 Samuel 31:1–6)

***

When David heard that Jonathan and Saul had been killed, he tore his clothes and wept. And he wrote this lamentation song to commemorate their lives.

The beauty of Israel is slain upon the high places:
how are the mighty fallen!
You mountains of Gilboa,
let there be no dew nor rain upon you,
for there the shield of the mighty is defiled,
the shield of Saul, as though he had not been anointed with oil.
Saul and Jonathan were lovely
and pleasant in their lives,
and in their death they were not divided:
they were swifter than eagles, they were stronger than lions.
How are the mighty fallen in the midst of the battle!
O Jonathan, you were slain in the high places.
I am distressed for you, my brother Jonathan:
very pleasant have you been to me:
your love to me was wonderful,
passing the love of women.
How are the mighty fallen,
and the weapons of war perished!
(2 Samuel 1:17–27)

Why I wrote this story

After King Saul was killed, David assumed the throne and became the most powerful and successful king in Israel's history. He also managed to get himself into some nasty scrapes, including the messy business of the rape of Bathsheba. The first child of that liaison died. The second was Solomon, who eventually became the second king in the Davidic dynasty – a king known, not for his military prowess, but for his great wisdom.

I'm not sure why my imagination made a link between the wisdom of Solomon and David's relationship with Jonathan. Perhaps it was because Solomon was noted for his wisdom, a feminine virtue in the Hebrew tradition. His way of ruling was radically different from most kings of his time. Solomon fought very few battles. He worked mostly to build up the economic and social infrastructure of his nation.

So somewhere in my head a spark jumped across a gap and I began to imagine that the love David and Jonathan experienced taught David that it was possible for men to love each other. There were other ways of relating besides competitiveness and killing. David didn't manage much of it in his life, but I thought perhaps he might have passed that learning on to Solomon.

There has been lots of speculation about whether the relationship between Jonathan and David was homosexual. There is no way of knowing. What I find most helpful is the relationship of love they shared, however they may have expressed it.

A deep and loving friendship with another man is an experience few of us men have, and we are poorer for it. Our friendships tend to be based on competitiveness rather than on openness and vulnerability. I found myself wondering what the story of King David, what the history of Israel might have been like, if the deep and loving friendship and commitment between David and Jonathan had been allowed to mature. Then I wondered if perhaps such thoughts occurred to David as he lay dying.

"A man is measured by the way he loves"

Some things are only known when people die.

Father lay there on his bed, shivering, trying to instruct me in the art of kingship. My mother was there too. She loved him in his dying as she had never loved him in his living.

"Have I apologized for what I did to you, Bathsheba? Have I?"

"Yes, David," said mother. "Many times in the last few weeks. And you are forgiven."

"I never apologized to Jonathan. I let him die there, slaughtered by the Philistines. 'How are the mighty fallen... how are the mighty fallen...'"

Father looked at me with dying eyes, but I could see a tenderness and longing there that I had never seen before.

"Did I ever tell you about Jonathan, Solomon? He was a fine man. If you think of yourself as a king, Solomon, you could do worse than look up to Jonathan. Did I tell you about him?"

"Yes, father." But I knew father would tell me once again. The matter of Jonathan seemed to be on his mind, persistent, unresolved, painful, and beautiful.

"Let him talk," my mother whispered. "Let him talk."

"Be sure to have the scribes write down the story of the battle at Gibeah, Solomon. And all the battles Jonathan fought. Write down how King Saul tried to have his own son killed because of some silly rule he made. 'No one eats till after the battle!' old Saul said. Jonathan never heard the order. He ate a tiny bit of honey and Saul would have killed him for that. 'We all took a vow and you broke it,' he said. When the boys in the army heard about it, well they almost staged a revolt. I would love to have seen Saul back off, humiliated – ha!"

Father tried to laugh, but choked instead and sputtered. Mother offered him some wine but he refused.

"And have the scribes write about the battle of Michmash, where Jonathan and his armor bearer climbed up through those ugly hills, and single-handedly killed 20 Philistines. All by themselves. That spooked the Philistines so much they turned and ran. They turned and ran because they thought my Jonathan was a giant. Well he was. Not outside of course. But inside he was big and strong – and warm and tender."

Father fell silent for awhile. There was softness in his eyes. And a tear. His hand trembled as he fingered the hem of his blanket.

"If only Saul..." and his voice broke. "If only Saul hadn't been so jealous...so sick. He was jealous of Jonathan, his own son. He was jealous of me because he thought I wanted his throne. I didn't want his throne. God had anointed him to rule, and I would never, never try to take that from him. Never.

"He tried to kill us. That business of eating the honey I told you about? It was a setup. I think he was jealous of Jonathan even then, because Jon was such a good fighter. He tried to kill me too—several times. If it hadn't been for Saul's jealousy, our friendship might not all have ended quite so soon.

"I could have killed him easily. So easily. Hey Solomon...your mother doesn't like it when I tell this story, but once when I was on the run, I was hiding in a cave. Saul and his men were right outside the cave, and Saul came in to the cave to take a leak. I was two feet from him and he didn't know. Did I ever tell you that story before, Solomon?"

"Yes, father."

"Hmmmmp. That's the trouble with being old, Solomon. I've told all my stories to everyone I know and nobody wants to listen to an old man's ramblings."

"That's not true, father. I like to hear you talk. Even if I've heard the story before, you sometimes add something new, a detail you hadn't mentioned before. There's something new each time. So please, keep telling me your stories."

Well, that wasn't all true, but I needed to keep on father's good side. He hadn't yet said officially who would succeed him as the king. My mother and I were determined to stay right there beside him till he made it official. I would be the king!

"Bathsheba? Do you know why I did that to you? Why I hauled you over to the palace here and raped you?"

"Don't keep punishing yourself, David," she said. "That is all in the past. You paid the price with grief and pain. Nathan saw to that."

"I almost forgot. Call Nathan," father said. "Send a message to Nathan to come here. Now." I left the room to send the message. When I came back, mother was crying and father was holding her hand.

"We both paid the price, Bathsheba, and it was all my fault. It started when Abner suggested I stay home from the war. I didn't like the smirk in his eyes when he said that, but he was right. I wasn't half the fighter I had been. And so I raped your mother, Solomon, just to prove myself a man."

"You are very much a man, David," mother said in her most motherly tones. "You are the greatest king in all of Israel, the greatest king in all the world."

"Saul could have been a great king if he hadn't been so jealous. If he hadn't been so sick. Jonathan would have been a great king too. We could have ruled together, he and I. What a great team we could have been. We'd have done it too, if Saul had let us. We had a pact, Jonathan and I. A covenant. I took his hand and he took mine, and we promised to love and respect and care for each other, till death do us part."

Father's eyes took on that softness once again. "Does that shock you, Solomon. It shocked old Saul. He called Jonathan some awful things. Awful things. But our love was good and beautiful and whole, Solomon. A man is measured by the way he loves, Solomon, not by how he fights."

Father began to weep. I had never seen him weep before. I don't know what to do with weeping men and so I moved away toward the window. Mother took his hand and stroked his hair with tenderness that grew through years of pain. Then in a cracked and tiny voice, my father sang:

> "The beauty of Israel is slain upon the hills:
> How are the mighty fallen in the midst of the battle!
> O Jonathan, you were slain on that hill.
> I am distressed for you, my brother Jonathan:
> very pleasant have you been to me:
> your love to me was wonderful,
> passing the love of women.
> How are the mighty fallen,
> and the weapons of war perished!"

I had heard the song before, of course. Many times. Father insisted that it be sung as a regular part of our Sabbath worship. And I knew father wrote the song when Jonathan and Saul were killed 40 years ago. But I had never heard it sung with such intensity – such power. Even in his old and squeaky voice my father sang with power.

"Solomon." Father broke into my thoughts. "Solomon, you will be king when I die. I have sent for the prophet Nathan who can look after the formalities. You will be a good king, Solomon. You will be a good king if you find a way to rule without the sword. It is possible for kings to love, you know. Jonathan and I discovered that. If you understand the wisdom of love, Solomon, you might find a better way to be a king."

Father took my hand and looked deep into my eyes. And then I knew my father loved me. He had never said it. I had never known it before. I didn't know that men could love each other – even fathers and their sons.

"Leave me now," he said. "I want to sleep." He looked so small and frail and weak. I knew his time was short.

My mother took my hand as we left the royal chambers. "Your father loves you, Solomon. I think he loves me too. At least a little. But he's never loved anyone the way he loved Jonathan. Not anyone."

Some things are only known when people die.

Tamar
a woman destroyed

Introduction

Tamar is one of the very few daughters of King David that we know anything about. There were lots of boys, and they made the "news" – the stories in the Bible – because they were men and they kept trying to kill each other and their father. But the women, with this painful exception, are hardly mentioned.

The story of Tamar is one of tragedy. It was never read much in churches during the Sunday readings because the story is embarrassing to men. It shows a callousness and cruelty and a double standard few of us want to admit.

Tamar was lured by her half-brother Amnon into a trap; he got her alone and raped her. Then he threw her out, like a piece of tainted meat and Tamar languished in Absalom's house. We hear no more about her.

The story in the Bible – *a paraphrase of 2 Samuel 13:1–33*

Absalom, the son of David, had a beautiful sister named Tamar. Amnon, her half-brother lusted after her. In fact, Amnon was so worked up, he got sick. Tamar was a virgin, and Amnon could not figure out a way that he could have sex with her.

Amnon had a friend named Jonadab – his cousin actually – and Jonadab was a very clever person. He asked Amnon, "How is it that you, the king's son are looking so thin and wan every day? Won't you tell me?"

Amnon said, "I love Tamar, my brother Absalom's sister."

"Well," said Jonadab, "Go to bed and pretend you are sick. When your father comes to see you, say, 'please let my sister Tamar come, and make some food for me here, and let her feed it to me.'"

So Amnon lay down and pretended to be sick, and when the king came to see him, he said, "Please let my sister Tamar come and make me a couple of cakes, right here while I watch her, so that I may eat out of her hand."

So David sent a message to Tamar. "Go to your brother Amnon's house and make him some food. So Tamar went to her brother Amnon's house where he was lying in his bed. She took some flour, and kneaded it, and made some cakes while he watched her. And she baked the cakes. Then she served the cakes to him but he refused to eat.

Amnon said, "Ask everyone to leave the house." Then he said to Tamar, "bring the cakes into my room so that you can feed them to me out of your hand. When Tamar brought the cakes into him, he grabbed her and said, "Come to bed with me, my sister."

She answered him. "No, my brother. Don't force me. Such a thing should not be done in Israel. Don't do this. Where would I go in my shame? And as for you, what would people think of you? Go talk to the king. He can arrange for us to be married."

Amnon wouldn't listen to her. He was stronger than she was, so he forced her and raped her. Then Amnon hated her with a hatred that was greater than the lust he'd had for her before.

Amnon said to her, "Get out of here!"

She said to him, "There is no reason for sending me away. This evil in sending me out of here is greater than the first evil you've already done to me."

Amnon paid no attention. He called one of his servants and said, "Throw this woman out and bolt the door after her."

Tamar was wearing a garment with long sleeves, because that's the kind of robes the unmarried daughters of the king wore. Tamar put ashes on her head and tore her garment; she put her hand on her head and went on crying.

Absalom her brother said to her, "Has Amnon your brother violated you? Don't go on about it, sister. He is your brother. Try not to think about it." So Tamar stayed on with Absalom – a desolate woman.

When David heard all these things, he was very angry but he did nothing because Amnon was his son. Absalom didn't say anything to his brother Amnon, either good or bad, though he hated Amnon because he had raped his sister Tamar.

Two full years later, Absalom had a big banquet – a party to celebrate the sheep-shearing. He invited David and Amnon and all the rest of the family, though David decided not to go.

Absalom gave instructions to his servants. "When Amnon has drunk enough wine that he's feeling no pain, go and kill him. Don't be afraid. I have given you orders."

When David heard about it, Absalom was banished to another country.

Why I wrote this story

Like everyone else, I like positive, happy stories. I resisted the story of Tamar because it is so painful. Perhaps that is why the story is not included in the lectionary (the schedule of readings for the church year) even though a group of women fought hard enough to have it included in the *Revised Common Lectionary*. It was only when I was writing the story of King David in the book *Man to Man* that I was forced to ask, "What does this story say to me?"

I like to read a chapter or two before and after a story in the Bible to find a bit of the context. And I was intrigued by the mention in the chapter following the story of Tamar that her brother Absalom names one of his daughters Tamar, and that she was known for her beauty (2 Samuel 14:27), just as her violated Aunt Tamar was known for her beauty.

If the younger Tamar, as she moved from childhood into womanhood, had talked with her Aunt, what might the conversation have revealed? The answer I imagined is pure fiction, of course, but it raised some very uncomfortable questions for me as a male – questions about the sexual violence women suffer at our hands, the double standard, and the ways in which these attitudes are carried forward into our children.

"Must the sins of the fathers be repeated by their sons?"

She stopped and kicked the dust with her sandal. A deep breath, then Tamar walked down the street toward her home. She had to know.

Without a word to the servant at the door, the thin, pale teenager moved down the corridor to a room she had known well but seldom entered. She knocked and opened the door. A thin, pale woman sat weaving wool, a woman old before her time.

"Why have you come, niece? You know I don't like visitors."

"I have to know. I have to know your story."

"It's over. And it's none of your business."

"My father named me after you, Aunt Tamar. I am your namesake. Some say I have your eyes, and they are beautiful. But whenever I ask about you, people turn silent."

"It's just as well. There is nothing to be said."

"My father announced my engagement yesterday."

"So? Congratulations, I suppose."

"When my father announced the name of the man I am to marry, my mother gasped and said, 'Oh, Absalom. What will Aunt Tamar say?'"

"Why? What business is it of mine?"

"I am to marry my cousin. Amnon's son Jonadab."

"Oh my God!"

"Why, Aunt Tamar? What is the story known to everyone but me? Please tell me. I am a woman now, and I have to know."

"Why did Amnon name his son Jonadab?"

"Jonadab was my uncle Amnon's best friend."

"Yes. I know." Suddenly her hands became busy at the loom. The shuttle fairly flew. Then just as suddenly she stopped. "Do you know why I never married?"

"No. Well, perhaps. The children in the street have taunted me. 'Tamar,' they say, 'have you been ruined like your auntie Tamar?' But I don't know what they mean. That's why I came. I want to know."

"Very well, my child. I didn't want to tell you this, but you are right. You are a woman now and you must know. It was years ago, and I too was dreaming of my wedding night. My father sent me word to go and make some food for my half brother Amnon because he was sick. If my father had not been so busy being king of all of Israel, he might have seen through the trick. But King David was like all the other men. He didn't really care.

"It was Jonadab who put Amnon up to it. Jonadab thought up the ruse. He suggested that Amnon feign an illness and ask for me to bring him food. And it worked. I found myself alone in a room with Amnon who grabbed me and threw me to the ground and raped me. I begged him not to. I told him he could marry me if he asked my father, David. I tried everything I could, but he was stronger than I. He hit me and he raped me. I wish he'd killed me."

The younger Tamar's eyes were wide with horror. "No wonder mother was upset."

"No, that isn't why. Amnon was a violent man, but worse, he was a cruel man. After he had raped me, he yelled at me, called me a 'dirty slut,' and threw me out onto the street. The law of Israel says that if he had sex with me, he had to marry me, but Amnon branded me a slut and threw me out.

"I had nowhere else to go but to my brother Absalom. Absalom told me not to worry. 'Forget about it, sis.' he said. How could I forget about it? I was a ruined woman. No one would marry me now. I would never bear children. I asked my father for some help. He was angry, but he wouldn't do a thing. 'Don't worry about it, Tamar,' he said. 'Boys will be boys, you know. I can't do anything about Amnon. He's my son, after all.' The laws of Israel do not protect the women, Tamar. Only men."

"So that is why you spend your days here, by yourself, spinning?"

"Absalom killed him. It took him two years to work himself up to it, but Absalom invited Amnon to a feast and got him drunk and killed him. He killed the man who would have been your father-in-law if he had lived."

"I knew my father killed Amnon. I never knew why. That must be why my mother is so upset. But father said he wants bygones to be bygones, and the dowry is so generous, he cannot refuse."

"No doubt. But child, that is not why your mother is upset. Amnon was a cruel and a violent man. I was not the only object of his cruelty. When he went in to see his wives and concubines, he would beat them, abuse them."

"But surely Jonadab will not be like his father! Surely not!"

The older Tamar saw herself reflected in the sad, dark eyes of her young namesake. She stood and walked to the casement window where the hot red sun was lowering to the west. Her niece watched patiently in silence till her aunt returned to sit before her loom and grasp the shuttle with whited knuckles.

"I will pray to God that Jonadab is good and kind, my child. I shall come to your wedding feast and I will rejoice with you. I will pray for you then – and always. And I shall weave a pure white wedding shawl to grace your deep black eyes. Now go to your own chambers. The day is ending."

"Thank you, Aunt Tamar," said the girl.

She glanced back at the older woman as she left, and knew she would return to talk some more.

She didn't hear the whispered prayer, "Oh God, must the sins of fathers be repeated by their sons? Must they?"

Naaman
because of a young slave girl

Introduction

Naaman may have been a nice person. At least, his name means "pleasantness." He was a commander in the Aramean army in about the 9th century, BCE, and he suffered from the dread disease of leprosy. Naaman's wife had a slave, a girl taken on a raid into Israel, who talked of a prophet called Elisha who could cure leprosy.

Naaman headed off to Samaria, a province of Israel, where he felt thoroughly insulted by Elisha who sent a note saying "Go bathe in the Jordan." Very reluctantly, Naaman went and was cured. In the process he came to believe in the God of Israel.

Healing of the soul so often comes with the healing of the body. And vice versa.

The story in the Bible – *a paraphrase of 2 Kings 5:1–15*

Naaman was chief of the army in Aram. He was a good man, and the king thought highly of him. God had given him a lot of military victories. But even so, he had leprosy.

In one of their raids into Israel, the Arameans had brought back a slave girl, who worked for Naaman's wife. "Wouldn't it be wonderful," said the slave girl, "if my master Naaman could see the prophet who is in Samaria. He would cure master Naaman of his leprosy."

Naaman went to the king and told him what the young girl had said. "Go," said the king. "I'll send along a letter of introduction to the King of Israel."

So Naaman put together a gift of silver and gold and fancy clothes. He took the letter to the King of Israel. "This letter is to introduce my servant Naaman. Please cure him of his leprosy."

The King of Israel was really upset. "Does he think I am God, that I can cure leprosy? Is this some kind of trick, to pick a fight with me?"

When Elisha, the man of God, heard how upset the king was, he sent a note: "Don't worry. Tell Naaman to come to me. He'll find out there are some real prophets in Israel."

So Naaman and all his chariots and horses went off to Elisha's house. Elisha sent out a message to him. "Go and bathe in the Jordan seven times. Your body will be healed and you will be well again."

At that, Naaman stomped off in a huff. "Doesn't he know who I am? He should have come out to greet me personally. He should have called on the name of his god, and done something dramatic to cure my leprosy. We've got far better rivers in my own country than this muddy creek they call a river. I could have washed in them and been healed!"

Some of his servants went up to Naaman when he had cooled down a bit. "Father, if the prophet had asked you to do something really hard and complicated, you would have done it. So when he suggests something this easy, why not just do it? What have you got to lose?"

So Naaman went and dipped under the water of the Jordan seven times, just as the man of God had suggested. His body was restored – like that of a young boy. Naaman was healed.

Then Naaman went back to the home of Elisha. "Now I know that there is only one god in all the world – the God of Israel."

Why I wrote this story

There are many themes running through the stories of the Bible. One of them could be called, "the least expected." Bev (to whom I am married) pointed out to me that the unnamed Israelite slave girl in this story was certainly "the least expected." Foreign, female, slave, and young. You couldn't get any lower on the status ladder.

I am convinced that God has a sense of humor. Army commanders and kings generally have a fairly high opinion of themselves. Naaman and his king were no exception. So when a Hebrew slave girl made a suggestion through Naaman's wife, the Commander had to swallow pretty hard. One of the gifts leprosy gave to Naaman was a touch of humility. Or was it desperation that forced him to pay attention to her suggestion?

Then Naaman had to take a deep breath and go to a country full of foreigners who had a weird language, who ate strange food, and who were generally considered inferior. When he got there, Naaman was really ticked off that the prophet didn't even come out of the house and perform some spectacular pyrotechnics. He sent a note. "Take a bath in the Jordan." I can understand Naaman's feelings. I would have felt slighted too. Maybe I have the same problem as Naaman.

Foreign slave girls, rude prophets, muddy creeks – God uses the least expected people and the most ordinary things to bring healing. Healing of the body sometimes, yes, but especially healing of the soul.

"That muddy creek soaked off his armor"

It was dark as pitch. Miriam lay on her mat, listening to her mistress toss back and forth in her bed in the next room.

"Miriam!"

"I'm coming, ma'am."

Miriam had been expecting the call. She had been called every night for months now. Her mistress would fall into a fitful sleep, then wake a few hours later, tense, tired, and frightened.

Even the smoky oil lamp seemed bright as Miriam emerged from the darkness of her little cell. "May I rub your back ma'am?" she asked.

"Yes, Miriam. Gently!" Ghazal's voice was tired. Miriam could hardly hear it, but it didn't matter. She had done this every night. Her strong, young hands moved firmly, gently along the knotted muscles in Ghazal's neck and shoulders.

Ghazal's shoulders sagged, relaxed just a little from the burden of fear. "It doesn't count for anything, Miriam. Not a thing."

"Ma'am?"

"Money. Status. Power. It doesn't get you anything in the end. They'll throw us away, like so much garbage. In the end, that's what will happen."

"Oh, ma'am. Surely not. Your husband is the commander of the army. He serves the king."

"Exactly!" Now there was anger in Ghazal's voice. "He serves the king. Naaman is commander of the army. The second most powerful man in this stupid country. And this man has leprosy! He has stinking, dirty leprosy! You know what they do with people who have leprosy, Miriam. As soon as it gets a bit worse, as soon as he can't cover that spot anymore, as soon as the wounds get ugly, they'll throw him onto the garbage heap. And me with him! Wives are attached to their husbands, so I go too. They'll send us out to live in the caves with the other lepers."

Ghazal's fury dissolved into tears – great screaming sobs that shook her whole body. Miriam's fingers continued their quiet ministry to Ghazal's aching shoulders, and the sobs moved into tears of quiet exhaustion.

"Oh Miriam, what would I do without you?" Ghazal reached back over her shoulder and took Miriam's hand. "Sit down, my child.

"How old are you, Miriam?"

"I don't know ma'am. I have been your slave for six winters since the warriors brought me here from Israel. I was very small then."

"You are old and wise beyond your years, Miriam. You are a girl-child, a slave, a Jew, and I couldn't survive all this without you. In your quiet way, you are wise. You seem to understand, and you seem to care about me. How can you possibly care about me, Miriam, when you are my slave and I have the power of life and death over you?"

The older woman looked deep into the dark, sad eyes of the girl. "Perhaps you are wise because you have suffered," said Ghazal. "You were ripped away from your home, your family. You have nothing left, except wisdom. Do we all have to suffer before we can be wise, Miriam?"

Ghazal began to cry again. "I've never suffered anything, Miriam, until now. I was a pampered child. I had wealth and power, or at least as much power as a woman can ever have. I never had to think or do anything for myself, Miriam. Nothing. I've never even had any children, so I don't even know what that is like.

"And now this thing with Naaman's leprosy. My whole world is coming apart, Miriam. They'll send Naaman away soon, when his leprosy spreads. They'll send him off, and then what's going to happen to me? I'll have to go and live in the caves with him. I can't survive in the caves with him. I can't live with him here, Miriam. He's so angry and afraid. He's always been proud and distant. Always the tough, aristocratic male. Now he's in pain and he pushes me away. You know, I haven't been in his bed for months."

Miriam nodded. Of course she knew. Miriam was a woman in a child's body. She stood up and went behind Ghazal's chair. Again, she massaged the burden from the knotted, hurting neck and shoulders.

"Ma'am!" Miriam said hesitantly.

Ghazal looked up at her.

"I'm sorry ma'am. I was going to say something but it is not my place to make suggestions."

"Miriam, if you know something that might help, please tell it."

"There is a prophet in my home place, a prophet of the God of Israel."

"What are you saying, Miriam? That he can cure leprosy?"

"I'm not sure, ma'am. I've heard it said."

"Do you think there's any chance, Miriam? Do you think there's any chance?"

"A great commander of the army would not accept the word of a Jewish slave girl."

"No, he wouldn't. Naaman is far too proud for that." Ghazal sat for awhile, the urgency, the desperation building inside her. "But he must. Leprosy doesn't respect commanders of the army. Naaman just has to get off his high horse and listen, even to the word of a Jewish slave girl."

For the first time in months, Ghazal stood up straight. She took the oil lamp, tucked her nightdress firmly around her, and walked toward the door leading to Naaman's bedroom.

Miriam went back to her mat. She was very tired. Through the small window of her cell she could see the first light of dawn.

***

It was light outside one morning when Miriam woke with a start. She had slept right through the night. She had not heard Ghazal stir, had not massaged Ghazal's shoulders, hadn't listened to Ghazal talk. Had Ghazal called and had she not heard?

Miriam rushed to Ghazal's bed. It was empty. It hadn't been slept in. For what seemed like an eternity, Miriam stood there at the bedside, wondering what had happened. What did the empty bed mean? Had Naaman come back? Her body rigid with fear, Miriam waited.

It was late in the morning when Ghazal finally came through the door. She was still in her nightgown. Her face was soft and she was smiling.

"Oh, Miriam. He's back. The leprosy is gone, Miriam. He did go to the Jordan river and he's cured." The older woman took the girl in her arms. "Thank you, Miriam."

There was a long silence, as the two women sat in each other's embrace. Finally Ghazal spoke again.

"We talked all night, Miriam. We really talked to each other. Among other things, of course." Miriam blushed and Ghazal chuckled.

"There's something that's been healed besides Naaman's leprosy, Miriam. I'm not sure what to call it, but it feels like a miracle. It was the "commander of the army" who went to Israel. But it was a man named Naaman who came back. He's a real man now, not just a swollen ego in a soldier suit.

"Naaman says that Jordan river of yours is just a muddy creek, Miriam. But maybe it soaked off his armor. Naaman says he did a lot of thinking along the way. I guess...I guess that God of yours knew that leprosy wasn't Naaman's main problem."

Jeremiah
a most reluctant prophet

Introduction

"Some are born great, some achieve greatness, and some have greatness thrust upon 'em."

William Shakespeare said that. I wonder if he was thinking of Jeremiah who certainly had greatness "thrust upon" him. His name means "God will elevate." He didn't much like it.

Jeremiah lived 600 or 700 years before Jesus and carried out most of his ministry in the city of Jerusalem. For a quiet, introspective country boy from Anathoth, that must have been hard. In fact, Jeremiah quite often complains of being called at the young age of 18. He would have understood Shakespeare's *Hamlet* who cried, "The times are out of joint – oh cursed spite / that ever I was born to put them right."

Jeremiah was not a popular preacher. People did not like what he had to say, and they told him so. Jeremiah took it very personally, but couldn't stop commenting on what he saw and speaking what he felt God called him to say.

Many modern prophets know exactly how he felt.

The story in the Bible – *a paraphrase of Jeremiah 20: 7–18*

O, God, you came after me, and I was talked into it. You had more power than I had, and so you won.

I'm the laughingstock of the town. Everyone makes fun me. Because whenever I speak, I just have to shout it out, "Violence and destruction!" God's word has brought me nothing but insults.

If I say, "I'll keep my mouth shut. I won't mention God—I won't even say God's name," then it feels as if there's a fire that burns inside of my bones. I get tired of trying to hold it in. I just can't do it any longer.

People talk about me. They whisper, "Look out! Report him!"

Even my best friends are just waiting for me to trip up. "Maybe we can get around him some way, then we can beat him and get even."

Never mind. God is a strong fighter and on my side, so the people who are trying to get me will fail. They'll be ashamed of themselves. They won't succeed. And people will never forget how they were dishonored.

Oh God, you put good people to the test. You can see what is going on in our hearts and minds. So let me see you get even with them, because you know I have been solidly on your side all along.

Sing a song to God. Praise God. God has helped people who are down and out and has protected them from evil folks.

I wish I had never been born. Don't ever celebrate my birthday. A curse on the man who came to my father and said, "Congratulations! It's a boy!" which made him very happy. I hope there's nothing but trouble for that man, because he should have killed me while I was still inside my mother. Why was I born? Just to see pain and suffering, and to spend my days in shame?

Why I wrote this story

A few years ago I saw a wonderful line drawing—an artist imagining what Jeremiah looked like. The portrait showed Jeremiah with a huge wooden yoke around his neck, one of the many symbols Jeremiah used to get people to pay attention. But the eyes! Jeremiah's eyes had that intensity that makes you say, "This man is either a real prophet or he is slightly nuts."

I had to write this story about Jeremiah for two reasons.

I have played the role of Jeremiah as an actor several times, and found the character complex, challenging, and quite upsetting. Jeremiah put everything he had and was into his faith. When I acted this intensity, some of it seeped deep enough inside to challenge my own lukewarm faith.

I had to get to know the Jeremiah in the Bible because I keep meeting real, live Jeremiahs in my work. When I travel around the country meeting with clergy to gather materials for the preaching periodical *Aha!!!*, I meet women and men who have that fire in their eyes – a light that I know shines up from the fire in their bellies.

That's not all the clergy I meet. Not even most of them. But prophetic leaders are out there, and I thank God for them, though

I find them just a little frightening. If you stand too close to that kind of fire you *will* get burned.

These people don't particularly enjoy being burdened with the message God has given them. They know full well that some people think they are on the wacko fringe. Maybe they are, but they have God's fire burning inside them, and they have no choice but to speak what they hear God telling them. And sometimes these prophets get really mad at God for not leaving them alone.

"A fire in my belly"

Look, Lord. I know I shouldn't talk to you this way. But we've had a pretty good relationship, you and I. Besides, I can't help it. I think I've been had. I think you, yes you, God, pulled a fast one on me.

I was just a kid, remember. Pink cheeks. No beard. And you grabbed me by the insides one day and told me to be a prophet.

Me. A prophet. I didn't even know what a prophet did. And I told you so, but oh, no. You wouldn't let me go. "I'll put the words right in your mouth," you told me. Do you remember that? I don't think you do.

I don't think you remember a bit of it because if those are your words, why doesn't anybody pay attention? Ha? Why do they all laugh at me, spit on me, call me names?

I use your words, God. *Your* words, not mine. "Violence and destruction," I tell them. "Violence and destruction unless you repent and do what God is asking of you."

I do everything I can think of to get their attention. I throw pots around, put a yoke around my neck. Once I even walked around naked. Stark naked, God. That got them talking, but not about my prophecy. They just wanted to send me to the funny farm.

Even my own family. They think I've flipped. They think I'm a nut case. It's not so bad when they yell at me, it's when they try to be kind and patronizing. "Now, just try not to get too upset, Jeremiah. You just need a little rest, that's all." Damn!

So for awhile, I didn't say a thing. Nothing. Quiet as a mouse. My mother loved it. You know what I got out of it. A sore stomach. A big old-fashioned gut ache. A fire in my belly that just had to get out. I couldn't keep quiet about the things I saw, I just couldn't. And you're sitting up there laughing at that, aren't you, God. You knew I couldn't keep it in.

Damn! I wish I'd never been born. I wish my mother and father had never been born. I wish I'd died while my mother was still pregnant. Damn!

So what do I do? You are God, and I'm just a poor underpaid prophet and I have no choice but to go with it. And it wouldn't be so bad if I didn't really believe those words you give me to say. I do, you know. You've taken over all right. You've taken over my head, and yes, even my heart. The plain unvarnished truth is that I really love you, God, and really do want people to hear what you have to say.

But I'm still mad at you.

Really mad.

And I'm going to stay mad just as long as I can, because being a prophet is no piece of cake. It's no walk in the rose garden.

Do you hear that God? Are you listening?

Mary and Elizabeth
good news and bad news

Introduction

Two pregnant women. One barely a teenager. The other a wise old crone. Good news for one. Terrifying news for the other.

Elizabeth, the mother of John the Baptist, had pretty well given up on having a child, when an angel came to her husband, the priest Zechariah, to announce it. The pregnancy was a great joy to Elizabeth. She had expected to die "unfulfilled," but now she was jubilant.

For Mary, the mother of Jesus, it was joy in the end, perhaps, but first it was real fear. Mary may have believed that her pregnancy was by the Holy Spirit but the people in Nazareth didn't. She was an unmarried pregnant teenager, and the punishment for that could be as severe as death by stoning.

Tradition says Elizabeth lived in Ein Karem, a village near Jerusalem, and only a few miles from Bethlehem. But for Mary to get there, she had a walk of several days from Nazareth.

The story in the Bible – *a paraphrase of Luke 1:39-56*

Mary left her home and hurried to a town in the hills of Judea. There she went into the house of Zechariah and greeted his wife, Elizabeth. When Elizabeth heard Mary call out to her, the baby leapt in her womb.

Filled with the Holy Spirit, Elizabeth shouted, "You are indeed blessed, Mary. The child you will birth is blessed too. I feel so honored that the mother of my Lord has come to visit me. When I heard the sound of your greeting, the child inside me leaped for joy. Mary, you are indeed blessed because you had the courage to believe what was spoken to you by God."

Then Mary sang this song:

> "My soul sings out in praise to God,
> My spirit sings joy to my Savior God.
> God looks kindly on my lowliness,

Surely, from now on, people of every generation
will called me blessed.
The Mighty God has done wonderful things for me,
Holy is God's name.
God's mercy is there for those who stand in awe
from one generation to the next.
God has shown strength, and scattered the proud
in the imagination of their hearts.
God has brought the powerful ones
down from their thrones,
filling the poor with good things
and sending the rich away, empty.
God has helped the people of Israel
to remember the mercy that was promised
to Abraham and his descendants forever."

Mary stayed with Elizabeth for about three months, and then
went back home.

Why I wrote this story

We were talking about maternity wards, and several of us older
men were saying how we envied younger couples having children.
"I wanted so much to be with Bev when our children were born," I
said, "and our doctor agreed, but the hospital rules said 'no.'"

One of the women in our group, an obstetrical nurse, didn't
say much for awhile. Eventually she sighed and chimed in. "It isn't
all joy and roses having the men there," she said. "A lot of them
are there because they think it's expected. Some hate it." Then she
blurted out, "You would be surprised how many children are born
to parents who don't want them."

We romanticize childbirth, generally, and the story of Mary and
the baby Jesus particularly. Men, I think, do it more than women.
Many women know it can be uncomfortable, often painful, and
always dangerous. It was especially dangerous in the year 4 BCE
when this all happened. Mary could have lost her life, if not from
stoning by the local authorities, then because so many women died
in childbirth.

Before the birth of Jesus was good news for Mary, it was very
bad news.

"The God who sang the song through you."

Mary's feet hurt. She'd forgotten how far it was from Nazareth to the hilltop home of her cousin Elizabeth.

Mary had started out early that morning, trying hard to hide her morning sickness. A desperate and fearful child she was – all of 14 years old, making up stories and excuses so she could go to visit her cousin.

Why Elizabeth? Mary wasn't sure. Except that Mary knew Elizabeth had always loved her even when she had felt less than lovable. And now, when Mary was in terrible trouble, she hoped – she knew Elizabeth would love her still.

Except that Elizabeth was married to a priest, and priests were sworn to enforce the very law that would surely have her executed. Death by stoning was the punishment for girls who got pregnant before marriage.

Now Elizabeth's house was just up the hill. And there was Elizabeth, big as life and pregnant.

"Elizabeth!" Mary called, joy and fear mingling in her voice.

"Mary!"

The two women ran toward each other, embraced and cried and laughed.

"Let me look at you, Mary," said Elizabeth, cupping her cousin's face in her hands. With her wise old eyes, Elizabeth looked deep into the young and tragic eyes of her cousin and saw the pain there.

"Mary, what's wrong?"

The dam burst. The flood of tears, held back by courage and by fear, burst and spilled into the arms of the older woman, who held the young one close until the flood had passed.

"I'm pregnant, Elizabeth," Mary whispered.

"Oh God, help us," said Elizabeth, not as a curse but as a prayer. "God, help us!"

"It's so hard to explain...," Mary began.

"Then don't explain, Mary," Elizabeth said, touching Mary gently on the lips. "Just know that regardless of what may have happened, I love you and God loves you. Now let's just sit down here, in the shade, and talk."

And talk they did. Until the sun had set and they pulled their cloaks around themselves against the cold, they talked as only women who know pain and joy know how to talk.

"Mary," said Elizabeth, "I could feel my baby kicking inside me when I heard you call. That baby was glad to see you, Mary. Glad to see you, and the baby you are carrying. Mary, a child to come is God's promise of hope."

"I know that, Elizabeth. There is one part of me that is strong and hopeful and full of joy. There's another part of me that is angry and terrified and cowardly. Sometimes I feel as if I'm two people."

"Mary, do you remember an old song I used to sing for you – the one that was sung so many years ago by Hannah, one of our foremothers, when she waited those long years for a baby? During all the long, long years I waited for God to send me a baby, that song helped me feel strength and patience, even when I was afraid and angry."

Quietly, then with more and more strength, Mary began to sing the old, old song.

"All that I am
grows and expands,
and rejoices with God
who will save me.
Small as I am,
I grow and expand,
to the future and God
who has blessed me.
God's love offers life,
God's strength is the love
that brings justice and peace
to all nations.
God's love offers life,
to the poor and the meek
who are raised from the ground
where they suffer.
All that I am
grows and expands,
with God who brings life,
hope and justice."

Elizabeth looked at the slip of a girl called Mary. So thin, so weak, so vulnerable. And yet, deep in those dark, youthful eyes, Elizabeth saw great strength, courage, and faith.

"I don't know how, Mary, because I know all the laws and all the customs of our people are lined up to destroy you. But somehow I believe God is with you. The child in my womb, the child in yours, are God's gifts of hope, Mary. Can you believe that? Even when everything seems to be painful and wrong, can you believe in the God who sang that song through you?"

Anna
the first Christian evangelist

Introduction

Anna is one of those fascinating shadows that flits across the screen. We catch a glimpse and she is gone. All we know is what is told us in three short verses of Luke. Anna was married for seven years, then widowed. From then on, Anna served full-time at the temple, praying and fasting. And when she saw the child Jesus, she immediately began to tell everyone who would listen that the Messiah, the "consolation of Israel," had arrived.

Anna was the first Christian evangelist. She was the first to proclaim the good news of the Messiah. The only other possible contenders for this title of first evangelist were the shepherds who visited the stable, but the text says they went home glorifying and praising God. That's celebration, but not evangelism. Anna went out and spread the word to the folks around the temple. She was the first Christian preacher.

The story in the Bible – *a paraphrase of Luke 2:25-40*

There was a man living in Jerusalem. His name was Simeon. He was a good man, who tried to do the right thing. And Simeon believed that God's promises to Israel would be fulfilled. The Holy Spirit rested with this man.

Simeon believed most firmly that he wouldn't die until he had seen God's Messiah. And so it was that Simeon, with the guidance of the Holy Spirit, came to the temple. When the parents of Jesus brought the baby to the temple to dedicate the child to God, Simeon took the baby in his arms and sang this song:

"Oh God, it's just as you promised.
Now I can die in peace.
With my very own eyes,
I have seen your salvation,
which you have brought to us here
and which is for the whole world to see.

This will be a beacon of light
for all the people of the world,
and a source of glory
for the people of Israel."

The child's mother and father were astounded at what Simeon was saying. Then Simeon offered a blessing, and said to Mary, "Many people will rise and fall because of this child. What he stands for will be seriously opposed, and in the process, the inner thoughts of many people will be revealed.

"And Mary," added Simeon, "sometimes it will feel to you as if a sword is driven into your heart."

Also in the temple was a prophet, Anna. She was the daughter of Phanuel and a member of the tribe of Asher.

Anna was very old. She had lived with her husband for seven years after they were married, but now she was an eighty-four-year-old widow. Anna never left the temple, but spent her time in prayer, day and night.

Just at that moment, Anna came and saw the child. Then she went around the temple talking to all those people who, like her, were hoping that God would come and save Israel.

When Mary and Joseph had done all the things that the law required of them in the temple, they went back to the Galilee area, to their home town, Nazareth. And the child grew strong and healthy. He was a wise child, and God's love was with him in a special way.

Why I wrote this story

When I closed my eyes and imagined what Anna might look like, I saw my Aunt Susie.

Aunt Susie was five foot nothing tall, with the most marvelously bowed legs, that had her walking in a duck-like side-to-side waddle. I would watch her for hours, swaying around the kitchen, when, as a child, I went to visit her and Uncle Henry on their farm.

Aunt Susie lived to a great age. But during her entire life I remember her being the caregiver. She was always cooking for someone, fixing something for me or for her daughters, always looking after people.

It wasn't surprising that when I saw Anna as my Aunt Susie, I then saw my Uncle Henry as crusty old Simeon. Then I began wondering what Aunt Susie would have done when she saw the young Mary and Joseph with the tiny infant coming into the temple. And if old Simeon really was ready to die, once he had seen the child of promise, how would Aunt Susie (Anna) have responded to that?

"I already know, old friend"

Her legs were bowed with childhood rickets and with 84 years of life.

"I walk like an old goose," she would cackle, "but in my mind, eh, in my mind I still soar like an eagle."

Sometimes Anna counted her years by the people she had survived. Five children she had borne, and outlived every one of them. She'd been the midwife who brought the High Priest of the temple into the world and she now acted as his unofficial "mother emeritus."

"Very unofficial," Anna grins. "His Highness doesn't want it known that I blew his nose and wiped his bum when he was a tadpole. But he comes and talks to me when nobody's looking. It wouldn't do for him to be seen talking to a woman, now would it?"

Anna had moved into the temple, expecting to die there soon. But death didn't come. Instead she found a new kind of life, a life of caring and counseling and friendship to the many people who came in and out of the temple each day. Her body grew smaller, her legs bowed a little more, but her eyes grew bright and gentle with wisdom and good humor.

Anna's special concern was for young families. Jewish custom required a first-born son to be brought to the temple and dedicated to God.

"Those parents – they're just children really – they're so frightened, so anxious. We've got lots of priests around here, but they're so busy being important, they don't have time for young families. So I just show them around and help them get things done."

Anna's special concern was for poor families, intimidated by the wealth and power of the temple, afraid of being cheated by the money changers – as they often were. Anna got them through. That was her mission. Getting them through a tough time.

But Anna had a secret dream. She hadn't shared it with anyone except her old friend Simeon. Anna and Simeon, like Jews everywhere, had been raised with the hope that someday God would send a Messiah, a chosen one, someone who would bring in a new era of love and justice.

"Do you suppose we might see God's chosen one?" old Simeon would ask. "Do you suppose it's possible?"

"I live in hope, Simeon. I live in hope."

"But how will we know, Anna? How will we know?"

"We'll know, Simeon," Anna said, then wondered why she felt so confident.

***

It was getting late in the day. Anna's bowed legs were tired. She'd been active all day in the temple, in her ministry of being there for anyone who needed her. Then she saw a frail, teenage girl carrying a baby. Beside her a man, slightly older. Anna walked over as quickly as her goose-like gait could carry her.

"Welcome to the temple, my children." She could see they were hot and tired from their long walk. "Come over here into the shade of the wall. You can rest for a moment. May I see your baby?"

It wasn't that the baby looked different than all the other babies brought into the temple. There was nothing unusual about the mother who held it. But there was something very different happening inside Anna, an exquisite ache, a sense of powerful weakness.

"Simeon!" The name was whispered, but with such intensity, the old man who was dozing nearby woke with a start. He hurried over to Anna.

Simeon looked at the child. He saw nothing unusual. But then he looked into the fire-bright eyes of his old friend.

"Anna? Do you suppose?" Her eyes answered his question.

Simeon began to sing. An ancient song, half remembered, half made up, a song of hope and thanksgiving, a song of pain and rejoicing. Anna, who had no voice at that moment, sang along in her heart.

"Dear God,
now I can die in peace,
as you promised.
I have seen your salvation
a gift to all people...

a light for the Gentiles
and glory for your people, Israel."

Late that night, Anna wept long and quietly. She grieved and celebrated all that was, and all that was yet to be. And then she slept.

It was only a few days later that Anna was midwife at another kind of birth. Her old friend Simeon was dying, and she was at his side, holding his hand and helping him through it, as she had helped so many others through life's changes.

"I think I can die now, Anna. I'll know very soon whether that child really is the Messiah, the chosen one. I'll know very soon." Simeon closed his eyes for the last time.

"But I know already, my old friend. Sleep well."

Simon Peter
Simon gets a new job

Introduction

Peter was part of a small fishing collective on what is usually called the "sea" of Galilee, though it is really a lake. He worked with his brother Andrew, and with Zebedee and his two sons James and John. All except papa Zebedee left the fishing business to follow Jesus. Peter and Andrew may have been disciples of John the Baptist before leaving him to follow Jesus.

Jesus used Peter's boat to speak to the crowds on shore. There are little bays on the north coast of the Galilee. Each one forms a natural auditorium, and made excellent teaching locations where Jesus could address the crowds that seemed to follow him everywhere.

That fact has affected the way we talk about our faith. Not the jargon of scholars and not the metaphors of trade and commerce, but the speech of the fisherfolk and their simple craft has become central to the language and symbol of Christianity. Along with the metaphor of shepherd, Jesus used the images he learned from Peter and the other fisherfolk who followed him and went fishing for the love that dwells in human lives.

The story in the Bible – *a paraphrase of Luke 5:1–11*

Jesus was standing beside Lake Galilee, and the crowd that had gathered was pressing in on him. They were anxious to hear the word of God.

Jesus saw a couple of boats near the water's edge. The fisherfolk were nearby on the shore cleaning their nets. Jesus got into the boat belonging to Simon, and asked him to row out just a little way from the shore. Then Jesus sat down in the boat and talked to the crowd.

When Jesus had finished his speech, he said to Simon, "Take your boat out into the deep water and let down your nets there."

"But Master," said Simon, "we've been fishing all night and

caught nothing. But if you say so, I'll do it."

When they had done what Jesus suggested, they caught so many fish their nets were starting to break. They waved to their partners on the beach to bring the other boat to help them. They filled both boats with fish to the point where they were ready to sink.

Simon Peter saw what had happened and fell down on his knees in front of Jesus. "Get away from me Lord. I am a sinful man." He was amazed at all the fish he had caught, and so were James and John, the sons of Zebedee who were Simon's partners in the fishing business.

"Don't be afraid, Simon," Jesus said. "From now on, you will be catching people."

When they had pulled their boats up onto the shore, the three of them left everything and followed Jesus.

Why I wrote this story

I met Simon once. In the flesh.

He was big and tall and bony, and he caught fish for a living on the Galilean Lake. He seemed so much like Simon Peter to me, that I can't remember his real name.

The man I met had left Poland as a boy, moved to Israel, where he fished the Galilee from the kibbutz En Gev. He was Jewish. But he made a lifetime hobby of studying fishing practices as they were described in the Christian scriptures. He had memorized all four gospels, in Hebrew, Polish, and English, and was an acknowledged expert on that subject.

We were a group of Christians, mostly Roman Catholic priests, studying in Israel, who gathered to hear him speak and show his slides. Half-way through his talk he dropped the tray of slides, flared in anger, then offered an expletive he refused to translate. Two minutes later he was laughing at himself. Working the projector was much too fine a work for his big working-person's hands.

This man cared, passionately and deeply, about the ecology of the Galilee and about the future of his country. Just like Simon Peter, I thought, who could do nothing by halves, and if it came to that, would die for his convictions.

Who else could I have in mind to give flesh and blood to the Simon Peter in Luke's story?

"Come and help me fish for people"

Simon was bushed. Dog tired. His shoulders hurt from rowing, his legs hurt from standing, and his throat was raw. He was catching a cold.

That was the good news. The bad news was that Simon hadn't caught even a minnow all night. "The place is clean fished out," he complained to nobody in particular. Simon often talked to himself. "Too damn many people fishing around here."

Nothing to do now but to clean the net. Get the weeds and the twigs and the junk out of it. "Thankless job!" Simon muttered. "Tomorrow I'll just catch more of this muck."

Head down into his net and into his dejection, Simon didn't see Jesus coming up the beach. But he heard the crowd of people with him and looked up. Simon knew Jesus. The Galilee wasn't such a big place that you wouldn't know him. Especially a strange one like this Jesus.

Not that Simon was glad to see him. Simon didn't have much use for preachers. "I'll do my fishin', they can do their preachin'," he would say. "Just leave me be, that's all."

"Simon," called Jesus. "May I use your boat?"

"I suppose," said Simon a little surprised. "Why?"

"If you stop it near the shore, I can sit in it and talk to the people."

"You mean you want me to row it out, and sit there while you preach at them people?"

"Do you mind?" Jesus smiled at him.

"Course I mind," thought Simon. He didn't say it though. He scowled and got into his boat and waited for Jesus to climb aboard. Then two or three strokes of the oars was all it took to get Jesus just enough away from the crowd so he could talk to them.

"Well, I'll row him out here, but I don't have to listen to his preaching," Simon thought. But gradually Simon *did* begin to listen. Simon found himself thinking thoughts that never occurred to him before. When Jesus finished speaking, Simon found himself wishing he would go on.

"Is that all?" asked Simon. "I was just startin' to get the hang of it."

"Well, I'm tired and they're tired," Jesus grinned. "Thanks for helping. How'd you make out with the fishing?"

That brought Simon back to reality with a thump. "Not a thing! Not a godd..." He caught himself. "Not a thing. The place is fished out."

"I think I can find you some fish," said Jesus.

"Oh sure," thought Simon. "Now this carpenter-turned-preacher thinks he knows something about fishing." But Simon didn't say that.

"Let's go where the water is deep," said Jesus. "Then try again."

Simon couldn't think of any way to get out of it. So he rowed out to the deeper water. "I'll go through the motions to satisfy this busybody," he thought.

"Holy mackerel!" yelled Simon when he started to pull in the net. It was so full, he could hardly get it in the boat. Heaving and hauling, he filled the boat so full there was some danger it might sink. And his tired muscles protested when he rowed toward the shore.

"That man is some preacher," Simon thought to himself. "And he knows fishin'. He knows people. He knows God. He knows fishin'. Some kind a man. Some kind a man."

Then the feelings of inadequacy, inferiority came over him in wave after wave of depression. "What does a guy with all those smarts want with me, anyway?"

Simon had his little speech memorized by the time he and Jesus pulled the heavy boat full of fish onto the shore. "Look, Jesus bar Joseph. You shouldn't be hanging around here with the likes of me. I'm not much good, see. I'm a working man. My language gets a little rough, sometimes. Can't keep up with all that religion stuff at the temple. So thanks for the tip about the fish. Help yourself to as many as you want. But I'll just get on with my work."

"Simon," said Jesus. "I helped you with your work. Why don't you come and help me with mine?"

"Look," said Simon. "All I know is catchin' fish!"

"Fine," laughed Jesus. "Come, help me catch people."

Simon looked down at his big rough hands. He looked up at Jesus standing there smiling, laughing. He looked at the people sitting in small groups along the shore.

"Well, maybe just for a bit," he grumped.

The Syro-Phoenician woman
educating the Messiah

Introduction

Jesus is in foreign territory. It seems he was looking for a little peace and quiet – a retreat we might call it. So he left his own country and went into the district of Tyre and Sidon, when he encountered the woman. Here the accounts in the two gospels differ a little. Marks says she was Greek by religion – Matthew says she was a Canaanite. She probably spoke to Jesus in the common Greek that was used in the region, which was a kind of *lingua franca* that Jesus probably knew as well.

Other than that, we know almost nothing about her. Not even her name. We don't know what the woman meant by an "unclean spirit." It may have been epilepsy. We do understand the fierceness of her love.

The story in the Bible – *a paraphrase of*
Mark 7:26–30 and Matthew 15:21–28

Jesus went off into a nearby country called Tyre. He took a room in a house and told everyone not to let people know he was there. But it was impossible to keep his presence a secret.

A woman, who had a daughter that suffered from an unclean spirit, heard about Jesus. She came into the house and kneeled down in front of him. The woman was not Jewish. She had been born in Syro-Phoenicia. "O Lord, you are the son of David, " she pleaded. "My daughter is terribly sick. She is possessed by a demon. Please! Make her well."

At first, Jesus ignored the woman. Then the disciples came along and wanted Jesus to order her to leave. "She's making a scene," they said.

Then Jesus said to her, "You have to let the children eat first. You don't take a child's food and give it to a puppy. I can't help you. I've been sent only to the children of Israel."

She responded. "That's true, Lord. But even the dogs under the table still get to eat the children's crumbs."

"A very good response," said Jesus. "You have a lot of faith. Because of that you can go home. The demon has left your daughter."

So the woman went home and found her daughter lying on her bed. The demon was gone!

Why I told this story

Traditional Christianity claims that Jesus was both completely human and completely God. If he was completely human, he didn't have all the answers, he could learn from others.

In a Bible study group a few years ago, one of the women got quite excited about this story. She saw in the Syro-Phoenician woman a person empowered by her desperation.

"I had a terribly sick child a few years ago," she said. "And I had an arrogant doctor. But he was the only doctor in town. I don't think I have ever been as sharp or as quick or as determined as when I was dealing with that s.o.b. doctor. There is nothing that strengthens a woman like fighting for the life of her child. That woman in the Bible story taught Jesus something about being the Messiah, just like I had to teach that man how to be a decent doctor."

When I read this story, I remember the fire in that woman's eyes.

"Even mutts get a few scraps"

"You can't go in there," said Peter.

"Well, I *am* going in there whether you like it or not."

"I said, you can't go in there, woman."

"I am going in, mister. I have a sick daughter at home, and I am going in there and that prophet of yours is going to fix her. Now get out of my way before I give you a swift kick in the shins."

Peter jumped aside. The fierce eyes of the woman frightened him. He followed her into the house. "I told her you didn't want to be disturbed, Jesus. But she wouldn't listen."

"Jesus? That's your name? They say you are a prophet. They say you are a very mighty prophet. Some say you are the Messiah. All right, I'm asking you. No, I'm begging you, Jesus, Lord, son of David, help my daughter. She is desperately sick with epilepsy. If she doesn't get help, she will die."

Jesus was sitting on a mat in a corner of the room away from the hot sunshine coming in through the window. He was meditating – trying to rest, trying to regain some strength after the exhausting work in Capernaum. Jesus was tense and tired and annoyed at the woman for intruding on his retreat. He kept his eyes closed, hoping she would take the hint and leave.

"Look, I'm sorry. But I need your help, Jesus. My daughter is dying and I *need your help!*"

"Just tell her to leave, Jesus," said Peter. "She'll listen to you."

"I can't help you. I'm sorry. That's just the way it is. I was sent to the people of Israel. To the Jews. Please leave." His voice had the edge of utter exhaustion.

"Surely, if you are a man of God, you have come to *all* of God's people."

"The children of Israel are God's people. Look, I'm sorry. But you don't take the bread that is meant for the children and feed it to your puppy, do you." Jesus smiled just a little during the last comment, perhaps to soften the insult. The smile gave her hope.

"Right," she said, her eyes flaming with desperation. "But even the mutts on the street get to eat some of the scraps off the family table. Surely, Jesus, your God has enough love to give a little to those of us who are not Jewish!"

Jesus recoiled a little. His hand massaged his forehead as if to ease a headache. He felt the woman's piercing eyes. Through his mind flashed the stories of his people, the wonderful humor of the parable of Jonah who was sent to bring God's message to the hated Ninevites, the moving story of Ruth, the foreigner, who became an ancestor to the great King David, and the stories his own mother had told him of his birth – of foreign Magi who came bearing gifts.

"You are right," said Jesus barely above a whisper. "Of course you are right. You are also very courageous. Go home. Your daughter will be well."

"Thank you," she said, and now her mother's tenderness went out to Jesus. "Go back to your meditation. You look as if you need the rest."

"Meditation, yes," Jesus said quietly. "You have given me much to meditate upon."

Pontius Pilate
they might have liked each other

Introduction

Pilate is one of those people about whom we know more than the Bible tells us. The Romans kept lots of records, so we know a great deal about this troubled bureaucrat.

Pilate was Procurator of Judea between 26 and 36 CE. His run-in with Jesus happened about the year 30. He was about the same age as Jesus. It's quite possible he got the job because of his wife, Claudia, who was higher up the social ladder than he was – an illegitimate granddaughter of the Emperor Augustus, no less.

Normally, Pilate and Claudia lived in the seaside town of Caesarea. But each year at Passover, they moved to the Praetorium in Jerusalem, because if there was to be trouble in the Jewish nation, it was likely to erupt during Passover.

Pilate did not like or understand the Jews or Judaism. And he probably didn't want to. Nothing would have pleased him more than if the Jews had simply run their religious affairs themselves and left him to govern the nation. But for Jews, there was no separation. Religion and politics were all one, and for Pilate, that meant nothing but trouble.

The story in the Bible – *a paraphrase of Matthew 27:11–23 and John 18:28–40*

Jesus was dragged before the governor.

"Are you the King of the Jews?" Pilate demanded.

"If you say so."

But when the chief priests and the elders accused him of all sorts of things, Jesus simply said nothing. Pilate tried again. "Don't you hear what they are saying about you?" Again, Jesus refused to answer, to anything. And this amazed Pilate.

There was a custom in Jerusalem for the Governor to release a prisoner during the Passover, to appease the Jewish crowd. And this time they had in mind a notorious crook named Jesus Barabbas.

When Pilate asked them, "Who do you want me to release to you? Jesus Barabbas, or the Jesus who they call the Messiah?" Pilate was well aware that it was mostly jealousy that prompted the priests and scribes.

It was still early in the morning. Pilate was sitting on his official chair outside his headquarters. A message came from his wife. "Don't have anything to do with that man. He's innocent. I just woke up from a terrible dream about him."

Then Pilate went inside his headquarters and ordered that Jesus be brought in to him. "Are you the King of the Jews?" he demanded.

"Are you asking this on your own? Or did those people outside put it into your head to ask me?"

"I'm not a Jew, understand. It's your own people and their chief priests that have handed you over. What have you done?"

"My realm is not the same as a kingdom in this world. If my realm were of this world, my friends and followers would be fighting with your soldiers to keep me from being handed over to those people out there. But that's not what I'm about."

"So you are some kind of king?"

"If you say so, I guess I must be. But I came into this world – I was born to tell people the truth. People who recognize the truth listen to me.

"Hah!" said Pilate. "What is truth?"

Pilate got up and went outside again. "I can't find anything against him. But you have a custom that I release someone during your Passover. Do you want me to release your *king*?"

While Jesus was inside with Pilate, the priests and the scribes had gone around and persuaded the crowd to ask that Barabbas be the one Pilate would release, and that Jesus should be killed.

"Speak up. Which of those two do you want released?"

"Barabbas! Barabbas!"

"Then what should I do with the other Jesus, the one who is called the Messiah?"

"We want him crucified!"

"Why? What has he done?"

"We want him crucified!"

Pilate realized he was cornered. He could see a riot starting. So he called for a basin of water and washed his hands in front of the crowd. "See! I am not to blame for the death of this man. It's your problem. Do it yourselves."

"We'll take the blame!" the people in the crowd yelled. "Blame it on us and on our children."

So Pilate signed the release for Barabbas. Then he had Jesus whipped, and handed over to the crowd to be killed.

Why I wrote this story

It was George Bernard Shaw, the famous Irish playwright. Shaw wrote many successful and memorable plays, but he wrote one called *On the Rocks* which bombed. In his introduction to the play (and Shaw's introductions were often longer than the plays) he presented an imaginary dialog between Jesus and Pilate. Shaw wondered what kind of discussion these two men might have had behind closed doors, away from the crowd in the privacy of Pilate's apartment.

Shaw was an atheist. Yet, he had a deep respect for Jesus and his teaching. In his dialog, Pilate, the career diplomat and bureaucrat, confronted Jesus, the visionary poet. And the two simply talked past each other. Both, from their own viewpoints, presented clear, valid perspectives. They could not hear each other from their solitudes.

I might have dedicated this whole book to them. While my sympathies are very clearly with Jesus, I can see the necessity from which Pilate operates. I too have been an administrator and a bureaucrat, though I don't think I was much good at it. Without administrators, things soon become chaotic and painful for everyone. Without visionaries, we become nothing but machines and there is nothing worth administrating.

Perhaps I should have dedicated this book to Claudia, Pilate's wife, who had bad dreams about this confrontation. People who pay attention to their dreams sometimes understand these things. That's why I imagined this story through her experience.

"They might have seen themselves as brothers"

I wonder, sometimes, if they might have been friends. If they had met in some other circumstance, I think my husband and Jesus might have liked each other.

They were about the same age. Both of them passionate, committed, opinionated. Bullheaded sometimes. And intelligent too, I think. Except they thought so differently.

Jesus was a Jew. Pilate was a Roman. And Pilate never understood the Jews, and that drove him almost to distraction. "You can't get a clear answer out of them about anything," he would fume. "Ask them a straight, logical question and they tell you a story, for gawd sake!"

Pilate wanted so badly to make a success of governing the Judeans. He knew perfectly well he would never have gotten the appointment as Governor if he hadn't been married to me, granddaughter of the Emperor Augustus. Even so, Judea wasn't exactly a plum appointment, insofar as these diplomatic posts go. But Pilate hoped that if he did this well, his next appointment would be to something he and I would both be proud of. Something a little closer to Rome, we hoped.

But things got off to a bad start as soon as we arrived in Judea. Pilate had a showdown with the Jewish leaders over whether Caesar's image could be displayed in the temple area. It was a dumb thing to fight about and Pilate knew it. "But I've got to show them I am strong and resolute, Claudia," he said to me. "If I show just a hint of weakness, if I back down even an inch, that snake of a high priest, Caiaphas, will take every slight advantage that I give him."

The showdown came when 7,000 Jewish men kneeled down in the market place, bared their necks, and dared Pilate to massacre them. Pilate folded. I don't think he ever really recovered.

Judea was a "no-win" situation for him. The bureaucrats in Rome just read the bottom line. Did he collect his quota in taxes? Did he avoid any embarrassments? If the answer was "yes" to those questions, you stayed on and maybe eventually got promoted to a better posting. If the answer was "no," you were recalled to Rome and sent to shuffle papers in an office somewhere. But Judea was so much more complicated than that.

Pilate tried. My gawd he tried. He read that blessed policy manual every night and memorized every procedure. But of course they never fit. "Who wrote this stuff anyway," he fumed. "I bet they've never been outside of Rome. They sure as hell have never been to Judea." And then he would throw the scroll in the corner and read the philosophy he loved so well—philosophy that seemed so clean and rational to him, and so unlike the reality around him in Judea.

And then the Jesus business broke. It was a recipe for disaster. Pilate couldn't win this one and I knew it. I even had dreams about it. "Get this man Jesus out of your life, Pilate," I said. "No matter what you do, you'll lose."

"I'll do what's appropriate and necessary, Claudia," Pilate said in his official voice, which meant that he was frightened. "I will interview the prisoner and judge him according to our Roman justice. He will be treated fairly."

"I know that Pilate, but that's not the game here."

"I'll decide what the game is, Claudia!" he said. And the conversation ended.

They brought the prisoner up to the praetorium. Pilate met them outside, a gesture of good will, so the Judean leaders wouldn't need to contaminate themselves, or whatever terrible thing is supposed to happen when they set foot inside a Roman building. He interviewed Jesus there in front of them.

"Look," he finally said. "The guy is just a little crazy, and yes, a bit of a trouble-maker. But he hasn't done anything to deserve execution. I mean, I can't have him killed just because you people don't like him. What I'll do is have him flogged. That'll straighten him out."

Well, you should have heard the hullabaloo. "We want him dead!" they yelled. "We want him crucified!"

Listen. Pilate has integrity. He's shown that before and he showed it then. He wasn't about to execute a man unless a crime had been committed, and blasphemy was no crime in Roman eyes. But Pilate was no fool either. He knew that Caiaphas had his ways of getting messages to Rome.

What followed was a mish-mash of political maneuvering, charges, and counter charges. I don't quite know what happened. I was in bed for most of it fighting off a migraine.

But I'll not soon forget what happened when Pilate dragged this Jesus up into our quarters so he could talk with him, away from all the yelling and screaming outside. That was when it struck me how alike they were, and yet how different. Two men of talent and integrity speaking to each across such vastly different realities.

In spite of all the pressure, Pilate still wanted to do the right thing. "Look," he said to Jesus. "Give me a reason, give me something that'll satisfy that mob – something I can put in my report to Rome so I don't have to have you killed." Jesus looked right back at Pilate – looked at – through him. But he said nothing.

Pilate lost his cool. "Look, I have the power of life and death over you. I can send you out to be torn apart by that mob, or I can save your hide."

"You have no real power over me," said Jesus. "No power that really counts. You and I are caught in this evil drama. You have your role to play, and I have mine."

"All right," said Pilate. "What's your role, except to satisfy the blood-lust of that mob?"

"I am called to live the truth," said Jesus.

"What is truth?" Pilate asked quietly, almost cynically. Jesus looked at him intently. And yes, compassionately. But he said nothing.

"Look, I asked you a question. What is truth?" Pilate lost his cool again. He paced around the room and banged his fist against the wall. But both men knew, I think, that Jesus could not reply in any way that Pilate could comprehend. Nor would Jesus have understood had Pilate defined truth for him.

The conversation stopped. There was nothing else to say. Jesus would die. And Pilate knew he'd spend the rest of his life rehearsing that conversation. "Why couldn't he just explain to me, logically and rationally, what he was up to?" Pilate asked that question over and over. "Those Jews. You ask them a question, and they sing you a song or tell you a story."

I too have rehearsed that conversation. I am back in Rome now, by myself. Pilate has been banished from the capital, not because of what he did to Jesus, but because of another diplomatic fiasco in Judea. Pilate did not understand the Jews.

And yet I wonder. If Pilate and this Jesus had met some other way, perhaps they would have learned to like each other – if they had had a chance to really talk, without the pressure. Pilate, the logical philosopher, might have discovered the poetic dreamer deep inside himself. And Jesus, the poetic dreamer, might have shown to Pilate the philosophy on which his dream was built.

There would have been respect at least. And just perhaps they might have seen themselves as brothers.

Mary of Magdala
dancing in the Spirit

Introduction

Mary of Magdala isn't mentioned in this story. You could argue that she wasn't even there on that first Pentecost when the Christian church was born. But Acts 1:13–14 tells us who was at that gathering. The apostles were there – the inner circle of Jesus' followers. As well as "certain women, including Mary, the mother of Jesus, as well as the brothers." And the first thing they had to do was to choose someone to replace Judas who had killed himself.

It's my opinion that Mary of Magdala was much closer to that inner circle than the story indicates. In fact, I think she should have been chosen as an apostle, rather than Matthias. She wasn't even nominated. But Mary was a strong and powerful leader in the early Christian church. She certainly qualified as an "apostle" and was far more instrumental in getting that first church started than we tend to acknowledge.

The story in the Bible – *a paraphrase of Acts 2:1–18*

When Pentecost day had come, all of the followers of Jesus were together in one room. All at once, from heaven, they heard the rush of a strong wind. The wind filled the whole house.

Tongues of fire could be seen among them. One of the tongues rested on each one of them. All the followers were filled with God's Spirit, and they began to talk in other languages, as the Spirit taught them how.

There were devout Jews, who had gathered from all over the world, living in Jerusalem. When they heard this sound, a crowd gathered. They were confused, because each of them heard the disciples speaking in their own native language. They were completely amazed, so they asked, "Aren't these people from Galilee? How come each of us hears them talking about God's deeds of power in our own native tongue?"

All of them were astonished, and they said to each other, "What does this mean?" But some snorted: "They're drunk!"

Peter stood up and began speaking. "People of Judea. Here's something you need to know. Please listen to me. We are not drunk as some of you say. It's only nine o'clock in the morning! No, this is what the prophet Joel was talking about when he said:

'In the last days, God declares,
I'll pour my spirit on everyone.
Your sons and your daughters will speak prophecies,
young men will have visions
and old men will dream dreams.
Even on my servants, both women and men,
I will pour out my spirit.'"

Why I wrote this story

Like many males my age, I'm pretty stiff when it comes to things like "speaking in tongues" and "singing in the spirit." And if (heaven forbid!) our minister should suggest that we get up and dance in church, I'd be the last one off my fanny.

There's one voice in my head that says, "C'mon! Loosen up, Ralph!" And an equally strong voice that says, "Don't make an ass of yourself." The second voice usually wins, at least when it comes to expressing myself through body language such as interpretive movement or dance. Verbally, I can be quite childlike and silly. But I do it with words I can understand, none of this "gibberish" and free-wheeling uncontrolled emotion. As for dance, well my shoes are nailed to the floor.

If you read the introduction to this book, you encountered more words than you probably wanted about "nonrational" expression. My head says one thing. My body another.

That's why I wrote this story. I wanted Mary of Magdala to get me (Peter) off my duff and out on the floor, dancing.

"This is it folks! This is IT!"

"Close the window, will you, John." There was more than a hint of irritation in Peter's voice. "All that singing out there is getting on my nerves."

"Peter," Mary said gently. "It is, after all, the feast of Pentecost. This is a happy festival. And they don't share our sorrow, Peter." Mary knew the sorrow as well as anyone. She had left her home in Magdala to follow Jesus to Jerusalem. She had watched Jesus wretch out his life on the cross.

"Right! But I don't have to listen to it," he snapped. "Any new business?" Nothing but gloomy silence from the group of men and women gathered there. They had gone through the unpleasant business of choosing a successor to Judas, the man who had betrayed Jesus. Now they had their full quota of 12 men, to match the 12 sons of Israel. Everything was neat and in order. And lifeless.

"So what do we do now?" John wanted to know. "Should we put up a monument or something. People are already starting to forget that Jesus even existed."

"Yeah," Philip agreed, but there was no enthusiasm in his voice. "Maybe we could collect some money and then put up a monument. A statue of Jesus. Or something."

The gloom hung like a damp cloud over the disciples – the women and men who were gathered together – the ragtag group of people who had known Jesus, who had loved him, who had heard his voice, who had felt and seen the hope for a new way of living together in love. And then they had watched him die. Some had seen a resurrected Jesus, but the others didn't really believe their story. Now they were together, a kind of memorial society for Jesus of Nazareth. Somehow it seemed important to stay together, but nobody really knew why.

"It's stifling in here," said Mary. Peter gave her an annoyed look as she got up to open the window. A cool breeze came in, along with the sounds of singing and the celebration of Pentecost from nearby homes. The breeze cooled Mary's face. That helped a little.

Mary began to sing. She sang an old song she had known since her childhood, a song she had often sung with Mary the mother of Jesus.

"My soul magnifies the Lord,
and my spirit rejoices in God, my Savior..."

She sang quietly at first, humming some of the parts, then louder, and it seemed that as she sang, the breeze from the window became stronger, blowing back her head dress, teasing her hair, lifting her spirit. She sang in a full-bodied contralto, a voice she hadn't used since that terrible day she watched her dearest friend cough and wretch and bleed and die.

"God has helped the servant Israel,
God remembers all the promises,
that were made to Abraham and to Sarah,
and to all their descendants, for ever,
and ever, and ever..."

"Sarah's not in the song. You're changing the words," grumped Peter.

Mary grinned at him. "She is now!" She hadn't felt herself smile for so long, and it felt so good. She sang the song, with her own new words, all over again, louder than before, and some of the other women joined in. And the next thing they knew, they were dancing.

They danced out the pent-up anger and grief and frustration and confusion. They danced out the hope, the tiny, fragile hope they still had in spite of all that had happened.

They danced and they sang. At first the men disapproved, then they began to smile, then some of them joined in the singing and the dancing. Even Peter couldn't sustain his grump. Even big, flat-footed Peter danced an awkward, joyful kind of dance and sang loudly off-key.

And the wind picked up and blew hard through the room. They opened other windows, they sang louder and danced their hearts out. Something was happening. Something electric. Something crackling with energy. Something had taken hold of their spirits and was moving them, motivating them.

Faces appeared at the windows. The door was opened. Curious neighbors looked in – neighbors and their guests who had gathered from everywhere for the feast of Pentecost. They saw the dancing and the singing, and the ecstatic laughter-filled attempts to explain what was happening, when nobody really knew what was happening. There were tears and there was laughter and the dancing got faster and the singing got louder until everyone collapsed into an exhausted, happy heap.

"They're drunk!" sneered one of the neighbors at the door.

"Ooo, no! Not drunk. Not drunk at all," laughed Peter, who in the end had danced as hard and sung as loud as anyone. "At least, not drunk on wine. Sit down folks, and I'll tell you what's going on."

"Do you remember the prophet Joel," he asked. The neighbors nodded. Of course. "Joel prophesied that the Spirit of God would be poured out on all people. 'Your sons and your daughters shall prophesy,' Joel said. And that's what you saw.

"Jesus of Nazareth. Do you remember him? He was killed. He was crucified. But he promised he would send the Spirit again in a new way. Well, this is it, folks. This is IT!"

And Peter began to dance again; to dance and to sing with a slow, awkward, passionate grace, with intensity and power and with a brightness in his eyes that literally sent shivers through the folks standing by.

***

They tried many times to describe what happened that Pentecost day. Some said they saw tongues of flame dancing over their heads. Others remembered speaking in strange tongues, or singing in strange tongues which everyone seemed to understand. Sometimes they would even get to arguing about what happened that day.

"My friends," Mary would interject when the arguments began. "Does it matter? We know the Holy Spirit came to us that day and filled us with excitement and love and passion. That's the part that's important. The Holy Spirit can come in a hundred different ways to many different people. It doesn't matter how. It only matters that we're open to the Spirit, and that we respond with our lives."

Peter
a saint in training

Introduction

Peter's name was Simon. But Jesus changed it for him one day, calling him Peter, which means "Rock," because that is exactly what Peter wasn't. Peter caught fish for a living, which meant he had a good, solid, respectable trade, but little in the way of formal education. He was probably illiterate. Still, he was part of Jesus' inner circle, along with James and John. According to the gospel of John, the first healing miracle that Jesus did was at Peter's house in Capernaum where he cured Peter's mother-in-law. And Peter's house became the base for Jesus' ministry around the lake of Galilee.

Peter was physically strong and emotionally volatile. And he suffered a bad case of "foot-in-mouth" disease – he would speak first and think second. And it got him into all kinds of trouble.

So perhaps Jesus renamed Simon, "Rock" (Peter), because he saw the potential in this man and sensed his profound friendship and loyalty. During the time when Jesus was in trouble with the authorities, when he was arrested and crucified, and even when he appeared to the disciples in Galilee, Peter kept messing up. And the only thing he could think of to do was to go back to his fishing.

But Jesus had promised help – not just for Peter, but for all his followers. And the help came at Pentecost, when Peter and the others found themselves profoundly charged with spiritual energy.

There is an ancient aphorism: "Gold must be tried by fire."

The story in the Bible – *a paraphrase of Acts 3:1–10*

Not long after Pentecost, Peter and John were on their way to the temple. It was three in the afternoon, the time for the prayer service. Some people brought in a man who was lame from birth. They put him at the entrance to the temple called the Beautiful Gate, so that he could beg for small coins from the people going in to worship. When the man saw John and Peter, he asked for money.

Peter and John both looked intently at him. "Look at us!" they commanded. The man looked back at them, hoping for a gift. Finally Peter said, "I don't have any silver or gold. But I will give you what I have. In the name of Jesus of Nazareth, stand up. Walk."

Then Peter took him by the hand and helped him up, and the man felt his feet and his ankles grow strong. He almost seemed to jump. He stood, began to walk, and went into the temple with Peter and John, where he too began praising God.

All the other worshipers saw the man walking and praising God. They recognized him as the beggar who always sat at the Beautiful Gate. They were astonished to see what had happened to him.

Why I wrote this story

They say preachers preach the sermons they need to hear. Certainly writers write the words they need to read. I am no exception in either case.

A few years ago in a restaurant with Kari, my daughter, I found myself in conversation with some people at a nearby table. I thought I recognized them. I didn't know them, it turned out, but that didn't prevent me from making some silly remark as I returned to the table.

"Dad," said Kari, "couldn't you develop a few inhibitions?"

It was at this same daughter's wedding that I blubbered through the entire ceremony. At Wood Lake Books where I work, I have a reputation for being disorganized and impetuous. I talk first and think second. When I do those personality profile things, I'm always shown as being "intuitive" or some variation of that theme.

Much of my personality is more traditionally feminine. At least, "cool hand Luke" is not a nickname they've ever pinned on me. Or Peter.

Which is why I keep going back to the stories of Peter in the Bible. Like Peter, I get into hot water because I shoot from the lip. Both of us live in a culture that values analysis, preparation, organization, planning, purpose, and cool detachment. "Stick-to-itiveness" my dad called it.

Simon didn't have it, so Jesus renamed him Peter and filled him full of boldness and spirit and enthusiasm.

I don't have it either. My name is Ralph which means "wolf" and that doesn't seem to help at all. But I have the story of my soul-mate Peter to infect me with his boldness, and to open my heart to that same Holy Spirit that filled Peter, so that now we call him Saint.

"I can't believe I did that!"

Peter and John hurried along the street. Life had been so busy for them since the Sunday of Pentecost. There were so many things to think about and do.

"That was quite a day," John was saying. "And that was quite a speech you made, Peter. Quite a speech."

"I still can't believe I said all that, Peter shook his head. "In front of all those people. Maybe I *was* drunk. I mean, where did I learn all that? All I know about is fishing."

"He was getting you ready," John said quietly.

"Who? What are you talking about?" Peter demanded.

"Jesus. Jesus was getting you ready to make that speech. Didn't you know that, Peter?"

"Make sense, John. I was the dumbest disciple of the bunch. I always had to ask Jesus three times before I got the point."

"That's just it, Peter. You asked three times. You kept asking until you understood. Some of the rest of us faked it. You kept asking. Maybe you weren't the smartest disciple, but you were the wisest. That's why Jesus called you Peter. The rock. Not brilliant. But faithful."

Peter thought about that as they walked along. The men were intent on getting to the temple for the hour of prayer. Peter couldn't remember when he had ever missed his prayer time. Even before he met Jesus, Peter went to synagogue regularly. Now it seemed even more important to pray every day.

"A few cents for a poor beggar!" The voice broke into their thoughts. "Just a few cents for a poor beggar. A few cents to buy a little food. Please!"

Peter stood for a long while looking deeply into the beggar's eyes. He looked at the man's lame leg twisted awkwardly under his body.

Peter took a long, deep breath. "Look at me!" Peter demanded. "I don't have any money to give you. But what I have I give. In the name of Jesus Christ of Nazareth, stand up and walk."

The man sat there blinking. He didn't move. Peter took his hand

and lifted. Gradually, the man stood up. He wobbled a little, then slowly, tentatively, he began to walk. Then to run. Then to yell and shout. "Look at me! I can walk! I can walk!"

"I don't believe it," said Peter. "I don't believe it."

"You don't believe what?" asked John.

"I don't believe I healed that man."

"You didn't," said John. "God did. But you were ready to be God's agent. You've been preparing all your life, Peter. And now you are ready to be the rock on which God builds the church."

Study Guide
finding new friends in the Bible

How to use this material in a Bible study group
or as a devotional resource

If you have not already done so, please read the introduction to this book. It will help you understand how we encounter the "word" of God when our experience resonates with the experience of others, particularly people of the Bible. That happens most effectively when we take the trouble to think and talk with others about our experiences and our feelings. That's one reason to gather in a study group, rather than simply read this book on your own.

Which is not to suggest that you shouldn't read this book on your own. In fact, you can use it as a personal study resource. A few hints on how to do that have been provided below.

If you have led other Bible study groups, you will soon realize that this one is *very different*. The purpose of this study is to learn about ourselves and to allow the Holy Spirit to speak to us through the Bible. The purpose is *not* to learn a lot of information about the Bible, but to find a way simply to enjoy it. And as a result, you may "fall in love" with some of the biblical characters. If that happens, more formal study will follow quite naturally.

Please remember an important point made in the introduction – that this study is about *nonrational* thinking, which is very different from *irrational* thinking. Please be ready at any time to become very rational and logical if someone becomes irrational. Nonrational thinking is a great and valuable gift, and it can provide the power in our faith. But like every gift, it has a danger. Give your imaginations free reign, but keep the rational part of you ready, in the background. Think of it as a parent listening in the next room.

Various ways to use this book

Don't be afraid to adapt the ideas in this study guide to suit your situation. Pick and choose from the many stories. You might use only the stories about men for instance, if you are leading a men's group, or only those about women for a women's group.

Some of the stories are seasonal. There are stories related to Christmas, Easter, and Pentecost. You might rearrange them so that the appropriate stories fall near the appropriate festivals.

You don't need to be limited to the stories told in this book. Once you've got the sense of how to imagine yourself into the stories, you can tell your own and do Bible study around the vast number of interesting characters in the Bible.

If you are leading devotions, you might pick the story that fits most closely with the theme of the meeting. If you are leading devotions several times during the course of a conference or assembly, you could pick the characters that fit the purposes or the theme of the gathering.

Or simply pick the ones you like best.

Leading a study group

Getting ready

When you advertise this study group, emphasize that people don't need to know *anything at all* about the Bible to enjoy this study, and they won't be put on the spot. They don't even have to believe anything in particular about the Bible to participate. They will get to know some of the exciting characters in the Bible and in the process learn a little about the Christian life and how it's lived. Nobody will preach at them. What they learn they will discover within themselves. And mention that there will be a lot of laughs.

In fact, you may choose not to call it a "Bible Study" at all, but something much more imaginative. One of these sessions was advertised as "Bedtime Stories for Big Kids."

It helps to put announcements in the church bulletin and newsletter, and to put posters on the walls. But enthusiasm can really only be communicated by live people who stand up in church and share their excitement. Personal conversations or phone calls with folks you think might be interested are the most helpful of all. This is especially true when the kind of group you are suggesting is very different from what people might be accustomed to.

As the leader, it's important to read the introduction to the book, and at least four or five of the stories before you even begin to advertise the sessions. This is a very different kind of Bible study, and you will not be able to explain what is going to happen unless you understand it yourself.

A skilled leader can probably adapt this material for any size group. However, a group not smaller than five and not larger than 12 is recommended. If more than 12 people register, find another leader and start another group.

People prefer to participate in a short series – somewhere between six and a dozen sessions. Pick the stories you like best and use them. If it's successful, you can do a second series with some of the rest of the stories. It's unrealistic to expect people to sign up for 23 sessions.

Many people prefer to meet in a home; it's cozy and it has less of a "classroom" feel to it. But you may also have very good reasons for meeting in a church.

Things you will need

1) If you have more than six or seven people, you will need to divide into subgroups during each session. Each subgroup will need a copy of this book. Please do not photocopy the material. That is both illegal and unethical.

2) Ideally, everyone should have a Bible, but as a minimum, have two or three Bibles for each group. Please use contemporary translations such as the *New Revised Standard Version* or the *Jerusalem Bible*. Please *do not use* the *King James* translation. People find it too hard to understand, especially if it's their first encounter with the Bible.

The sessions

1) Take time to make people comfortable. Use name tags at least during the first gathering, since it's unlikely everyone will know everyone else. Introduce people to each other as they come in, and do your best to stimulate "small-talk." Some groups find that serving coffee, tea, and juice at the beginning helps people feel more relaxed. Others prefer it at the end. Suit yourself. *(10 to 15 minutes)*

2) It is hard to say exactly how long each of these sessions should last. Discuss this with your group during the first session. *Remember*: it's far better to wish the discussion had gone on longer, than to wish it had stopped some time earlier. As P.T. Barnum often said, "Always leave 'em wanting more!" Many experienced study group leaders feel an hour and a half is about right. Emphasize gently but firmly that it is important to start and finish at the time agreed upon. *(10 to 15 minutes)*

3) Begin by explaining some of the things this Bible study *is not*. It will be very different than conventional Bible studies and hopefully a lot more fun. It will not be a history lesson. While participants may learn some bits of history, that's not the main purpose. The group will not try to learn "what the Bible says." The Bible "says" a great many things and the group will discover some of them as they go along, but that's not the main purpose.

The main purpose is to hear what God is saying to us through our imaginations and through the imaginations of those in the group as they allow themselves to become part of the stories in the Bible. God will speak to the group as it identifies with some of the characters in the Bible and as it imagines what they might be like and what they might have to say to the group.

Talk generally (in the whole group) about some people you and they have known personally. Be ready to share one or two stories from your background to prime the pump if necessary. Try to get people to talk about personalities, and how God creates us in such a wide variety. Wonder out loud together about why God makes each person unique, and what a wonderful gift this uniqueness is. (*About 15 minutes*)

4) Talk about one or two of your own favorite biblical characters. The characters you choose can be ones you plan to deal with in this study series, or others. Invite (but don't push) people to talk about any of their favorite Bible characters. Don't go around the circle or use any other technique that puts people on the spot, because many, perhaps most, of the people in your group may not know any Bible characters, or know so little they'd be embarrassed to talk about them.

Talk generally about what you find interesting in these characters. If someone has a particular interest in a biblical character, and that story is in this book, you might include that character in your series. (*From 5 to 15 minutes*)

5) Mention that the Bible is not primarily a rule book or a history book. It is a book of stories about people. They were *real* people – not alabaster saints. This Bible study is simply a way of getting to know those people and allowing them to talk to us. To do this, the group first needs to make connections with these biblical characters. The idea is to develop a relationship with those characters and to learn from them.

Talk about this concept with the group so they will feel free to do the imagining that will help them learn to enjoy the people of the Bible. Once again, the purpose of this study is to gain insights about ourselves, not to gather facts about the Bible. (*From 5 to 15 minutes*)

The above steps will be necessary during your first meeting and it is entirely possible you may not get to the steps that follow in the first session. No matter. Be sure you have a flexible plan to suit your particular group.

You may have to repeat some parts of steps 1–4 during the second or third meeting, especially if you have some people who did not attend the first session. In subsequent sessions, you may only need to use the following steps.

6) Take two or three minutes to introduce your first character from the book. Use material from the section titled, *Introduction.* You may wish to supplement this with any research you've done in your church library or your minister's library, but this is by no means necessary. Please don't lecture. Ask if anyone else in the group has anything to say about the character.

7) If you have more than seven people in your group, divide into subgroups of four to six people. Make sure each group has a couple

of Bibles and one copy of this book. Give the groups about 15 minutes to do the following four things:

a) Have someone read out loud the paraphrase of the story as Ralph Milton has written it under the heading, *The story in the Bible.*

b) Have someone else read the same story from the Bible itself. Ralph indicates at the top of each paraphrase, exactly where you can find this story in the Bible. Every Bible has a Table of Contents in the front so you can find the page number for each book.

c) Talk to each other about what kind of a person this character is. Use your imagination. Play detective and look for clues about the person in the story.

d) Does the biblical character remind you of anyone you know? Who? In what ways?

8) If you divided into subgroups, ask people to come back together into the whole group. Do a simple guided meditation. Explain that this is not a test. There are no right or wrong answers. Invite people to be like children playing "pretend." Ask people to make themselves comfortable and to close their eyes. Then, with a good pause between each phrase (about a slow five-count), say in a quiet and gentle voice:

♦ Imagine that you can see (insert the name of the biblical character, for example, Hagar). What does (Hagar) look like? (PAUSE)

♦ How old was (Hagar)? (PAUSE)

♦ What color were (Hagar)'s eyes? (PAUSE)

♦ What was the texture of (Hagar)'s skin? (PAUSE)

♦ What kind of clothing is (Hagar) wearing? (PAUSE)

• What attracts you to (Hagar)? (PAUSE)

♦ What don't you like about (Hagar)? (PAUSE)

   (*Note*: Use the character's name each time, rather than "he" or "she.")

9) Again, in the small groups, ask people to describe their impression of the character. Emphasize that there is no right or wrong in this. Participants are not trying to find out what this person *actually* looked like historically, but how they *imagine* that person to be. Two people could have totally opposite impressions, and both of them are "right." Invite people to enjoy the varying descriptions. Don't try to reconcile them, and be especially careful not to argue about them. (*From 5 to 15 minutes*)

10) Call attention to the comments from the book under the heading, *Why I wrote this story.* Make it clear that the story they are about to read or hear is *Ralph's* story about the Bible story. (Only take a minute or two for this unless someone has a real problem they need to discuss.)

11) Have someone read Ralph's story to the whole group. (*This will take anywhere from 2 to 20 minutes. You may want to designate someone in advance. Have them time the story when they rehearse it so you can adjust your plans accordingly.*)

12) Invite people on another guided meditation. If you have experience with guided meditations, you will want to use your own words. Otherwise, say the following in a quiet, gentle voice, allowing a full 10-15 second pause between each statement:

♦ Make yourself as comfortable as you can, close your eyes, and go with me as we pay a visit to (insert the name of the biblical character, for example, Hagar). (PAUSE)

♦ Breathe normally. Be aware of any sounds around you. Be aware of your body feeling relaxed and easy. (PAUSE)

♦ In your imagination, leave this place, and find yourself walking down a familiar road or pathway. (PAUSE)

♦ Notice the familiar things along the way. (PAUSE)

♦ Now you enter a familiar building. You have been here before and you are comfortable being here. Inside this building, you discover (Hagar) sitting waiting for you. (PAUSE)

♦ (Hagar) speaks your name and invites you to sit. As you sit down beside (Hagar), you realize there is something you'd really like to talk over with (her). You talk to (Hagar) as you would talk to a long-time friend.

♦ *Here, allow at least three or four minutes of silence.*

♦ Now, as you are ready, say goodbye to (Hagar). (PAUSE)

♦ You walk out the door of the familiar building, then slowly back down the familiar road. (PAUSE)

♦ When you are ready, come back into this room, and slowly open your eyes. (PAUSE)

13) Have the small groups discuss whatever they wish. If a participant's conversation with a character was confidential, they should simply say so and the other members of the group will respect that. If there are parts of the experience participants can share, please encourage them to do so. Remember, there are no right or wrong answers or responses. Simply encourage each participant to share whatever they feel moved to share. (*Allow up to 30 minutes for this, but keep an eye on the groups. If the conversation runs down, move to the next section.*)

14) In the larger group, allow people to talk about whatever they have on their minds. However, you might stimulate the conversation with questions such as the following: Did (Hagar) become more real to you? Is the situation Ralph Milton described anything like situations you have now encountered? Did anyone *not like* (Hagar)? How did

you feel about that? What did you learn from this encounter with (Hagar)?

15) If you have time, read out loud the story of the specific character, this time from the Bible itself. Remember to use a modern translation. Close with comments such as these: "God has given us such friends from the Bible. These biblical friends, with all their strengths and all their weaknesses, can walk with us in our life's journey. Such friends do not have all the answers, but they are there for us when we need them."

(5 to 10 minutes)

16) Say your goodbyes and remind people of the place and time of the next meeting. Or, invite people to have another "cuppa whatever," and do what it is you enjoy doing at such times.

17) During the final session, you might ask people to reflect on the differences between the various biblical characters they encountered – which one they like best or least, who was most helpful. Just for fun, you could give people a box of crayons and paper, and invite them to do a portrait of this character. A good question to ask is, "In what ways was (Hagar) like you?" And, if possible, have a little party to celebrate your new friendships.

Other ways to use this book

As a simple meditation

Sometime you may be asked to lead a meditation or worship service with a small group. A simple way to use this material in that setting is to select the character appropriate for the group or occasion, and then read *The story in the Bible...* from this book. Or you could read that part out of the Bible itself. Then, after telling people that this is an imaginative retelling, read Ralph's version of the story. You might choose to close with a short prayer.

In large groups

It is possible for seasoned leaders to do guided meditations even with very large groups seated in rows. In some situations, it would be best to do only the guided meditation that encourages people to visualize the character (See Step 7, p. 189). But some people have successfully led groups as large as several hundred through the guided meditation that encourages a conversation with the character (See Step 11, p. 190). If people are in table groups, it's also possible to discuss the guided meditation when it is finished. (See Step 12, p. 190).

In a worship context

You might expand the "simple meditation" (Step 7, p. 189) with any or all of the elements of a worship liturgy. Laypeople leading worship have used Ralph's stories as the "sermon." It is important in these situations to practice carefully so that the reading retains its dramatic power. Nothing can kill a story as quickly as a dull and lifeless reading, or one in which the reader stumbles frequently.

As preaching materials

Almost all the biblical stories told here appear in the various lectionaries. In fact, a few of Ralph's versions of the stories first appeared in the periodical *Aha!!! – the preacher's research assistant.*

As private meditations

How you approach this will depend on your needs and the time you have available. A variation on the group study process outlined above could be used privately – take yourself on your own guided meditation and reflection.

Few people would want to take an hour and a half at each such session. But if you devote ten minutes, for example, to such a meditation, you might consider spending several days or a week getting to know each biblical character. Read the introduction and paraphrase one day and allow the character to simmer in the back of your mind as you go about your day's events. The next day you might read the story in the book. If you are so inclined, you might sketch or paint a portrait of the biblical character. Most useful, perhaps, is to take the time to write a story about that character – one that connects with something in your life.

Remember to enjoy it

Whatever you do with this material, please remember that the most important element is your enjoyment. If you are enthusiastic and enjoy it yourself, the people you lead will soon share that feeling.